The Adventures of an Ordinary Pilot

by

H. C. "Skip" Smith

To my good buddy Jack Conrad, for all the memories of flying and other activities that we share.

Skip

DORRANCE PUBLISHING CO., INC.
PITTSBURGH, PENNSYLVANIA 15222

The contents of this work including, but not limited to, the accuracy of events, people, and places depicted; opinions expressed; permission to use previously published materials included; and any advice given or actions advocated are solely the responsibility of the author, who assumes all liability for said work and indemnifies the publisher against any claims stemming from publication of the work.

All Rights Reserved
Copyright © 2012 by H. C. "Skip" Smith

No part of this book may be reproduced or transmitted, downloaded, distributed, reverse engineered, or stored in or introduced into any information storage and retrieval system, in any form or by any means, including photocopying and recording, whether electronic or mechanical, now known or hereinafter invented without permission in writing from the publisher.

Dorrance Publishing Co., Inc.
701 Smithfield Street
Pittsburgh, PA 15222
Visit our website at *www.dorrancebookstore.com*

ISBN: 978-1-4349-2543-5
eISBN: 978-1-4349-2147-5

To my father, Col. Chas S., my hero, mentor, and best friend.

Acknowledgements

I would like to thank all my flight instructors and check pilots over the years, particularly my first instructor, the late Grant King, for providing me my aviation knowledge and skills. I also thank all my old wives and girlfriends who endured some less-than-ideal flights to accompany me on my aviation escapades. Special appreciation goes to Dr. Barnes W. "Barney" McCormick, former colleague and department head, who afforded me the opportunity to indulge in many of the adventures described. I would also be remiss if I didn't recognize the help given with the cover art and the editing by my friend April Gunsallus.

The Adventures of an Ordinary Pilot

by

H. C. "Skip" Smith

Introduction

Aviation adventure stories are usually written by test pilots, fighter aces, aerobatic champions, bush pilots, and the like. But all pilots experience adventure to some degree. Indeed, it has been said that every flight is an adventure. The very acts of lifting off the ground into the sky and then smoothly alighting back onto it lend an air of romanticism to this incredible phenomenon of flight. Encountering and dealing with non-forecast weather, unexpected traffic, or unusual field conditions present challenges, and thus add to the adventure of flying. Even on the most routine flights, however, soaring along thousands of feet above the ground, taking in the incredible sights below, and maneuvering at will to better view them, pilots share a unique experience. Hence, even the most ordinary pilot experiences adventure. This is the story of one such pilot—the adventures of an ordinary pilot.

Chapter One
The Beginning

On a bright spring day, a few months before I was born, my father somehow convinced my mother to take an airplane ride. It was her first and only flight, ever. For me, however, it was just the first of many more to come, and the spark that ignited within me a lifetime of passion for aviation.

My dad was, at the time, dean of Beckley College, a small private business and technology school in Harrisburg, Pennsylvania. In the late 1920's, the president instituted an aviation program that included flight training, and my dad was put in charge of this activity. In addition to his administrative duties, he learned to fly himself, mostly in the school's Fairchild Challenger.

After I was born, my dad used to circle over our house and wave, and my mother would hold up my little hand, and wave back to him. She soon concluded, though, that this was too risky an activity for a new father to pursue, and persuaded him to give up flying now that he had the responsibilities of fatherhood. Nevertheless, I grew up among pictures of airplanes on his study walls, many of them showing him in helmet and goggles in an open-cockpit biplane. It was also the "golden age of aviation," with frequent news about the exploits of Charles Lindbergh,

Jimmy Doolittle, Amelia Earhart, and other famous flyers. I couldn't help but be intrigued by flight.

Then, when World War II broke out, my dad accepted a direct commission into the Army Air Corps. He was too old for military flying by then, but his administrative experience was considered valuable. This move provided me with even more opportunity to connect with aviation. He was stationed at nearby Olmsted AFB, and often took me along to the base, and let me see the latest bombers and fighters close up. I even got to climb through them occasionally. It was a thrilling experience for a young boy.

I began building model airplanes at about the age of nine, and reading all sorts of aviation magazines. In my early teens, I even built a wood and cardboard mockup of an airplane fuselage large enough that I could sit in. It had complete and realistic moveable controls, and a panel with mock instruments. I called it the PS-1, for pursuit, by Smith, number one. I would sit in this, slide the cardboard canopy over my head, and imagine that I was a fighter squadron leader. I bought a book on how to fly, and made each flight as complete and realistic as I could. I would push the throttle in, raise the tail, then ease back on the stick to lift into the air. On returning to the airport, I would circle for the approach, and flare into a three-point landing. I had many an enjoyable hour in this fantasy.

I had several buddies who also were aviation fans, and we started a summer ritual of riding our bicycles to the nearest airport to watch the airplanes take off and land. It was called Wilson Field, and it was ten miles away. It took us just about an hour to get there. The Civilian Pilot Training Program was in full swing there at that time, so there was a lot of activity. It was also an era when we kids were welcomed onto the field, and allowed to look into the airplanes and sit under a wing to watch the flying. Those were magical days!

I didn't undertake actual flight instruction until my senior year in college. In my teens, I had considered myself still too immature for this challenging task. We had an ROTC instructor, however, who was an Air Force captain and pilot. One day in class, he announced that he had secured the use of a C-47 transport at the nearest Air Force base, Olmsted. The following Saturday, he planned to take any cadet who was interested on an orientation flight. I was among the first to volunteer. So, that Saturday, we loaded onto a bus and rode over to Olmsted AFB. There, we were fully briefed, issued a parachute, and we climbed aboard the transport. We sat on bucket seats along each side of the cabin, the way that paratroopers ride to the jump site.

Once we reached a few thousand feet, we leveled off, and one by one, we were ushered into the cockpit. We each climbed into the right seat, and were given the controls for a few minutes. When it was my turn, I eagerly grasped the control wheel, and proceeded to feel out the airplane. I knew basically what to do, but it took a while to get the feel of it and hold it straight and level. Once I felt comfortable, I made a gentle turn to the left, and then to the right. I couldn't believe I was actually flying this big twin-engine transport!

When I climbed out of that seat, I knew my life would never be the same. I had to learn how to fly. I looked up an old boyhood chum who had become a pilot, and flew out of Hackenberger Airport, a little strip to the northwest of Harrisburg. He was towing a glider for a guy who flew there on weekends, and also owned the tow plane, an old Navy N3N biplane. I went up that Sunday, and once he got the glider launched, he came down, handed me a helmet and goggles, and I climbed into the front cockpit. This time, I got to fly a bit more than in the C-47, and it also had a control stick and left hand throttle—just like my old PS-1!

I was now thoroughly addicted, and the next week went over to the old airport we used to ride to on our bikes, now called Taylor Airport (for the new owner), and inquired about lessons. I was introduced to the flight instructor, Ulysses Simpson Grant King, Jr. (imagine signing all that in a log book endorsement). Grant, as he was known, turned out to be a gem of an instructor. He had been an Army Air Corps instructor in WWII, and continued to pursue this profession in civilian life. He had no aspirations to move up to airline or corporate flying; he was a dedicated career instructor. On top of that, he was one of the most pleasant and genuinely nice guys you could meet. He told me just to call when I wanted to fly, and he would try to fit me into his schedule.

The next Saturday, the weather looked good, so I gave him a call, and he had an opening at 1:30. I took it. He showed me the various airplanes they used for training, but suggested that I train in their Piper J-3 Cub to get a more basic foundation. I later saw that this was excellent advice.

We walked all around the airplane, and he showed me the various features as well as what to check on the preflight. Then I climbed into the rear seat, and we taxied out. The Cub was soloed from the rear seat, so you trained in that position. Grant did much of the flying on this first lesson to demonstrate various techniques, but I got to handle it a little. When we returned, I had to purchase a logbook, and he made the first entry: "Piper J-3 N70824, 30 min. dual, familiarization, USG King, Jr." (So that's how he wrote it.)

When I got home, my parents were out shopping, so I proudly laid the book on the coffee table, open to the first entry. When they got home, my dad was elated. He shook my hand, hugged me, and verbally expressed his pride. My mother was much less enthralled, but she tactfully refrained from saying anything, not wishing to ruin this moment of bonding between a father and son.

I was pretty busy finishing up my last semester of college, but I managed to get in a few more lessons before it ended. After graduation, I had nothing to do but wait for orders to active duty. I had been commissioned into the Air Force Reserve upon completion of ROTC, and had a two-year active duty commitment. Until then, I dedicated my full time to flying. I went to the airport every day that the weather was fit, sometimes even taking a lesson in the morning and another in the afternoon.

My dad worked in Washington in those days, and only got home on weekends, so I would call him and keep him updated on my progress. I remember specifically telling him that I took off one day. In that lesson, I had taxied out, did the run up, and got ready to go. "Now, have you got a good tight grip on that stick?" Grant asked.

"Yep," I replied.

"Okay, then, let go, take a nice easy relaxed grip, and we'll proceed to take off," he told me in an easy, soft tone. That was his style, and it was very effective.

Grant required all his students to be able to recover from spins before they soloed, so the pre-solo work involved a lot of spin training as well as shooting landings. One day while spinning, I noticed bits of something yellow flying around the fuselage, and I thought pieces of the fabric were peeling off the yellow Cub. I quickly recovered, and then noticed that Grant was sitting up there peeling an orange, and tossing them out the window. It was his lunchtime.

I soloed on the fifth of June, just about a month after my first lesson. The first solo did not seem particularly dramatic to me. I just made one circuit of the pattern, and it didn't seem much different from dual, except that the airplane was much lighter. I became more aware of my solo status on the first trip out of the pattern. As I looked down at the farm fields on my way to the practice area, all of a sudden I realized that I was all alone up here. I would have to do everything alone, even finding my way back to the airport. Once I got into practicing the maneuvers, though, my apprehension went away, and I got back safely.

A few days later, I had another minor scare. I took off for a similar mission, and as I climbed out, something seemed wrong. The airplane didn't feel right. I was climbing, the engine sounded okay, and the instruments indicated normally, but something was different. Then, it struck me! The air was perfectly smooth. It was fairly early in the morning on a calm, overcast day, and I had usually gotten to the airport in the late morning when the thermals were acting up. I had gotten used to bouncing around, and had never flown in smooth air. I laughed at myself, as I realized that this was the way it was supposed to be.

Then came cross-country flying. The Cub was well equipped for cross-country navigation—it had a compass. No gyros, no radio, not even an electrical system. Everything was done by pilotage, and on our first trip—to Easton, PA—Grant told me to draw a line on the chart to the destination. Then he showed me how to take up headings, until, by trial and error, you found one that would keep you on the line by reference to landmarks on the ground. After the first 20 miles or so, he turned it over to me. About two-thirds of the way on the 100-mile trip, I looked back, and Grant had dozed off. (The student sat in front when nav was a major factor.) I assumed he had faith in me to get us there, which I did. The next day, I made the same trip solo, but dog-legged to York, and then back home. I got a little disoriented (lost) a few times, but always managed to get back on course.

The next trip served a dual purpose. In our flight to Hagerstown, MD, we continued to get cross-country experience, but also, I made my first landing on a paved runway. Up until then, all flights had been from grass-field airports. Grant kept cautioning me to be alert on the rudder pedals, even in the final flair, and his coaching worked. The airplane was a lot less stable on the ground, but I managed.

The following day, I started over the same course solo, but continued on to Martinsburg, WV, another hard-surface airport. I landed near the end of the runway, as I had been taught, and then found I had a long way to go to the FBO (fixed base operator), which was at the opposite end of the field. It seemed as if I taxied almost as long as I had flown.

I went in to order fuel and get my logbook signed, as was the custom in those days (to prove that you really were there), and they asked me to also sign the visiting pilots' register on the desk. When I picked up the pen and looked at the book, I saw the last signature was that of Arthur Godfrey, the famous radio and TV talk show host, who was a big booster of general aviation. He had been there earlier in his Bonanza. Wow, I was to sign next to Arthur Godfrey! I had made the big time. I was a real pilot now!

After a few more cross-countries, and some advanced maneuvers, it was time to take the private pilot exam. I first had to go to the CAA (Civil Aeronautics Administration, now FAA) office in Harrisburg and take the written test. The written test in those days consisted of twenty-five questions, all selected from a list of

200 that were published in a CAA guide, along with the answers. It was easy to read through these and remember them. I made 100 percent, and figured that only a sixth grade dropout could flunk this exam.

Grant was a designated examiner, and in those days, he could give the practical (flight) test to his own students. We scheduled the test just as an outsider would, and he had me run through the various maneuvers methodically, and scored me against the established standards. Even though I was his student, he was very professional, and treated me like any other applicant. When we got back, he signed my log, and wrote, "Private pilot test approved," and issued me a temporary certificate.

I was now a private pilot! It was July 11, two months and one week since my first lesson, and I had a total of thirty-five hours. Two days later, I took up my first passenger: my dad! I made a few more flights the following week, and then I had to report to Lackland AFB in Texas for active duty. My flying took a hiatus.

My dad when Dean of Beckley College with the school's first airplane.

My first picture in an airplane at the age of one.

Building models at age twelve.

Ready to "fly" the PS-1, my homemade airplane, in my early teens.

Chapter Two
Ownership

After several months at Lackland AFB in Texas, I was transferred to Olmsted AFB, in my old home area, for a six-month on-the-job training assignment in aircraft maintenance management. After that, I would probably be sent to the Korean area for service in the war. I was close enough to my old airport, though, to resume flying there. I flew the old Cub, and checked out in a Cessna 140, a Luscombe, and a few other similar airplanes.

Before my six-month OJT was completed, however, the Korean War ended, and it looked as if I would remain at Olmsted for the remainder of my active duty tour. I decided to look for an airplane to buy. The anticipated big boom in light aircraft ownership after WWII never developed, but there were thousands of light airplanes produced, and were now available at bargain prices.

I narrowed my search down to an Aeronca Chief. This was a side-by-side airplane, with a fairly plush interior, and, more importantly, had an adjustable seat. This feature was particularly necessary to accommodate my small frame. I couldn't reach the rudder pedals on many models. Besides, it just sort of stood out to me.

One day, a guy from Hanover, PA, flew into our field with a very nice Chief. It was in almost like-new condition with only 300 hours on it. I made him a generous offer, but he didn't want to sell. I gave him my card, anyway, and, a few months later, he called and said he was going into the Marines the next week, and would take $700 for a quick sale (I had offered him $800). I bought it! The price was a bargain, but not as cheap as it sounds today. That figure was a third of my annual salary at the time.

I picked up the airplane a few days later when a friend flew me down to Hanover. I was never so proud of anything in my life. I had my own airplane! It cruised about 85 mph, and had a range of a few hundred miles. In those days, we usually just flew around to nearby airports, and dropped in to see what was happening at that field.

One day, while just cruising around, I realized that I was near the farm home of a girl I had a crush on. I dropped down low, and circled her house, gunning the engine to attract attention, but she never appeared. A week or so later, I was sitting at the counter of the local restaurant hangout, when I heard two guys a few stools away talking. "Did you hear what happened to Jake Weaver's chickens?" the one guy asked.

When his buddy said no, he said, "Some nut in an airplane buzzed his farm, and now none of the chickens will lay eggs."

I sort of had a vague recollection of seeing chickens nearby when I buzzed the girl's house, so I waited until they left, and then asked the waitress where Jake Weaver's chicken farm was. She told me, and it was right next to the house I was buzzing. *Son-of-a-gun, that was me!* I thought. I never said a word about that incident to anyone in my hometown, even to this day.

I did occasionally make some trips in the Chief, especially to the Jersey shore, when my girlfriend at that time (not the one near the chicken farm) seemed eager to ride along. I thought that she liked to fly, but many years later (we remained friends over the years), she informed me that she hated it. She only went along to please me. Who knew? These trips, though, made me long for a faster, better-equipped airplane. The bug had set in.

After I was separated from active duty, I decided to try the aerial photography business. I had done part time pro photography since high school. I bought a second right-hand door from a salvage company, removed the glass, and cut it down like the open door of a Piper Cub. I bought a surplus military aerial camera, but found a 4x5 Speed Graphic press camera to be more appropriate. I hired a pilot to fly while I shot out the right opening.

After a few months, I quickly realized that this was a money-losing activity, so I decided to use my GI bill and return to school. I had worked with aeronautical engineers in the service, and found this to be a fascinating field. I made an appointment with the department head of the Aeronautical Engineering Department at Penn State University, and flew up to see him in my Chief (about 60 miles). Even in the Chief, I found the 45-minute trip to be a big advantage over the two and a half hour trip up through the mountains by car.

It turned out that the department head had always aspired to fly himself, and when he learned I had flown up in my own airplane, he was impressed and took an interest in me. He accepted me into their program, and worked out a schedule so that I could get a second degree in engineering in two or two and a half years. Flying was pretty much put on hold while I pursued this intense program.

When I graduated in 1959, Olmsted AFB had just been given some new activities that included an engineering department, and they were looking for several aeronautical engineers. I got one of the jobs. It was a perfect fit for me, and again allowed me to fly back at my old airport where my airplane was still hangared.

Unfortunately, that same year, the Chief did not pass annual inspection, and needed to be completely recovered, a job as expensive as the price I had paid for it. I decided that this was a good time to sell, and look for something a little more upscale. In the meantime, I rented again, and checked out in a Champion Tri Traveler (also, my tricycle gear checkout), a Tri-Pacer, and a Cessna 172, all fairly new aircraft.

There was also an Ercoupe dealer at the nearby Skyport airport, and they were now selling the new Forney Aircoupe. The original Ercoupe had a two-control system, where the control wheel moved both aileron and rudder together, as well as the nose wheel. I had always sort of shied away from this airplane, but now, there was a version of the Forney that had conventional controls. I checked out in one of these, and found I liked it very much. I had already been sold on tricycle gear, but this also had a low wing, which I liked just as much. I decided to look more closely at these airplanes.

Of course, the Forney was new, and hence, very expensive, but the dealer told me there was a rudder pedal conversion kit that could be put into the old ones. Great! I started to seek used Ercoupes, and found one at the Harrisburg Airport (now Capitol City) that was really sharp. It had highly polished natural aluminum, with a bit of attractive trim, an electrical system, lights, and a Narco Superhomer nav/com. I made a deal and bought it for $3,300. I then took it to Skyport, and had the rudder pedal kit put in. That was another $100.

The catch was that the pedals only moved the rudder; the nose wheel was still controlled by the control wheel. So, on takeoff, you had to keep it straight on the runway with the wheel, and then, as the speed picked up, you felt your feet become effective on the pedals. Still, it was a pretty good airplane, and I got used to this system.

My most memorable trip in the Ercoupe was a weekend vacation at the Jersey shore. I was dating a secretary in our office at the time, and she was anxious to make a trip to the shore, specifically, Wildwood, NJ. One week in the summer of 1962, the long-range forecast predicted a big high to settle in the following weekend for three or four days. We made plans to fly down to Cape May Co. Airport, close to Wildwood, that Thursday. We were all set—almost.

On Monday evening, a violent storm spawned a tornado that went right over the airport. One hangar was totally destroyed. The Ercoupe was in the newest concrete block hangar, which survived, but the storm lifted the roof off, and then dropped it back on, braking up much of the wooden structure. The pieces of 2x4's rained down on the airplanes inside. Fortunately, my low wing airplane was tucked in under a Cessna 172, a Cessna 195, a Stearman, and a Staggerwing Beech, which took the brunt of the damage. All that happened to the Ercoupe was a few little dents on the upper cowl.

The next day, I went over to the airport, as wrecking crews with big cranes were hard at work removing the rubble and the hulks that once had been airplanes. When I was able, I crawled into my hangar to survey the damage more closely. I was afraid that, in moving the other airplanes, further damage might occur to the Ercoupe. I persuaded my friend, Dick Chestnut, a mechanic at the airport, to remove the wings, and roll it out before they started on the others. He agreed, and we successfully did this. I remember taxiing the ship down to a good hangar with only the stubby center-section for wings. I informed Dick of my plans for Thursday, and asked if they could reassemble it by then. He assured me it would be ready.

Thursday was bright and clear, as forecast, so I took off work at noon, and headed for the airport. Sure enough, the airplane was all back together. I carefully pre-flighted it, gassed it up, checked the oil, etc., and went over the flight plan. My friend only wanted to take off work on Friday, so she worked until 5:00, and then had to go home and pack and get supper. By the time she got to the airport, it was 7:00 in the evening. We took off shortly afterward.

Crossing the Delaware into New Jersey, I noticed that it was getting to be dusk, so I switched on the navigation lights. In a few seconds, I detected a strong odor of burning wires. I thought that it was probably the lights, but, not wishing to take any chances, I immediately shut off the master switch. The odor cleared up, but now I had no lights or radio. I had a good heading established, though, so I pressed on.

By the time we neared Cape May Co., it was totally dark. The airport had no tower, but I assumed they expected pilots to call in, and at least announce position on Unicom. I couldn't, of course. I could see other airplanes entering the pattern to land, though, so I just followed after the last one, and proceeded to land. I wasn't even sure what runway I was landing on, but it was obviously the active one.

The airport was well lighted, including the taxiways and the ramp. I taxied to a parking spot with no trouble, and shut down. I fully expected to be chewed out by someone for landing with no lights or radio call, but, apparently, no one even noticed. I tied down for the night, and called a taxi to go into Wildwood.

We had an enjoyable few days, despite my friend's penchant for amusement rides, obviously her desire for this location. I was less enthralled by such activity. I regarded roller coasters and Ferris wheels as thrills for little kids. Mature guys drove sports cars and flew airplanes.

I made sure to leave well before dark, actually right after lunch. I did venture to turn on the master and the radio, which seemed to give no trouble. The flight home was routine. I taxied right to the shop, and informed them of the problem. They took a look, and, sure enough, someone forgot to slide the insulating sleeve over the navigation light connection in the left wing, and it was shorting against the metal structure. It was fixed in a few minutes.

Unfortunately, the mechanical condition of the Ercoupe was not quite as good as its appearance. Dick, the mechanic, informed me one day that the engine really needed a top overhaul. That winter, I took it over to the dealer at Harrisburg Airport, where I had bought it, and had the job done. After that, the engine ran fine—when it started. The engine was very difficult to start once it was warm. For the first flight of the day, it started up easily, but when I flew somewhere, and wanted to return, I had to crank and crank to get it started.

I had three different mechanics work on this problem, and each felt they had corrected it, but it still persisted. I was getting tired of this airplane because of this, and other chronic maintenance problems, so I put it up for sale. Once, I flew it down to Baltimore to demonstrate it to two guys who were interested in it. One got in to go up with me, and, of course, it wouldn't start. He got out, talked with his partner, and then came over to me, and said, "If you get it started, just take it home. We don't want it."

I had some further work done, and really thought I had corrected most of the problem. I pursued selling, though, and another partnership of two guys from New Castle, PA, flew in to look at it. I gave them each a demo ride. Of course, it was cold when I started it to take the first guy up. I just let it idle as he got out, and the second partner got it, so it continued to run fine. They made an offer of within $200 of what I had hoped to get for it, so I took it. One condition, though, was that I would deliver it.

The next Sunday was bright and clear, so I arranged for a buddy who flew the Olmsted Aero Club T-34 to pick me up, and headed out to New Castle. That was about 185 miles away, so it was a long trip. I packed a lunch, which I ate on the way. The buyers met me, we completed some paperwork, and then exchanged a bill of sale for a check. My buddy, Bob, had arrived in the meantime, so as I climbed into the T-34, I noticed the new owners had boarded the Ercoupe, and were cranking it up. As I watched them turn it over and over, I told Bob to hurry up and get out of there. As we climbed out, I could see them still cranking it over. I fully expected a call when I got home, but I never heard from them again. I really hope they got it straightened out and were happy with it.

In the coming months, I turned my attention to getting a new airplane—hopefully, a more capable one. For some reason, I had gotten interested in the early Bellanca Cruisairs, and started searching for one. There was an old Bellanca dealer at Lunken Airport in Cincinnati, who continued to sell used ones after factory production ceased. He had one advertised, so on the next business trip to Wright-Patterson AFB, I arranged for him to meet me at a small airport south of Dayton one evening.

He had a pilot pick me up in a Tri-Pacer and fly me down to Lunken. There, he showed me the airplane, which he was actually brokering, and said the owner, a young lawyer, would be out shortly, and take me for a ride. Pretty soon, a guy rode up on a motorcycle wearing a tuxedo. It was the lawyer. He spoke with a slight British accent, and seemed to be in a big hurry. He took me for a short ride, and said, "It's a good airplane, and very reliable. The engine only ever quit on me once, but I was able to put it into a field."

Very reassuring. He then told me to negotiate the price with the dealer, and asked to use the phone to call his lady friend so she would be ready to go to the opera. He then sped off on the bike. I had visions of a woman dressed in a gown straddling the back of the bike, and heading off with him for an evening at the opera.

Bellancas had manually retractable gear, which took thirty-four turns of a crank to raise it. There was, however, an electric gear conversion that was fairly popular, and I saw one with this mod advertised in Dallas. I had a trip near there a few weeks later, so I diverted down to Dallas, and arranged for the guy to fly into Love Field, the main airport there at the time, and give me a demo.

He had installed a doorbell as the gear warning device, and as we taxied out, the bell dinged every time we hit a seam or bump in the taxiway. It reminded me of the Good Humor trucks that used to go through the neighborhoods selling ice cream. After we ran up, the tower cleared him for takeoff, but he replied that he preferred to wait until the wake from a recently departed 707 had dissipated. After a minute or so, the tower called and asked if he was ready to go. He replied that he wanted to wait a little longer, and calmly sat back in the seat, while I nervously eyed several airliners waiting in line behind us.

The next one I looked into belonged to a doctor in Chicago. I called him and inquired about it. He sounded like a grumpy old codger. When I asked him if it had electric gear, he replied, "Anybody who is too damned lazy to crank up the gear shouldn't own a Bellanca."

I took it from that response that it didn't. I was beginning to think that Bellanca owners were a strange lot, and I was losing my enthusiasm for this airplane. I also became aware that early Mooney Mark 20's were selling at reasonable prices. The first Mooneys in the late 1950's had wooden wings and tails, and became somewhat obsolete when the all-metal version came out in 1961. The real reason, though, for my interest in this airplane was that it was much more modern than the Bellanca in both appearance and equipment, as well as having better performance.

My search turned to the Mooney, and I located one that had been just rebuilt at a major used aircraft dealer in Indiana. A 1958 model, it had all new paint in current style (1963), a complete new interior, and a newly majored engine. The dealer offered to fly it in and demonstrate it to me. I took one look at it and immediately fell in love. After some dickering, we settled on a price of $7900, a bargain for that airplane, but almost equal to my annual salary. Nevertheless, I scraped up half the money from the sale of the Ercoupe and some other savings, and financed the rest.

I had never flown a retractable gear airplane before, but I decided to try flying it myself, since there was no instructor with Mooney experience on the field. Fortunately, I did take my mechanic buddy, Dick, along. The Mooney had manual gear also, but it was actuated by a lever, which was much handier and faster than a crank system. I practiced raising and lowering the gear before attempting a landing. Finally, I decided that I had it down, and entered the pattern for a landing. As I retarded the throttle, Dick said, "Maybe we should think a little about the gear position."

I then realized that when the gear lever was up and latched under the instrument panel, the gear was down; when it was down on the floor, the gear was up, counter to logic. I had left it up. I quickly corrected, and never made that mistake again.

Amazingly, I was covered with insurance for this first flight, even though I had no retractable experience. Imagine insurance companies doing that today! I later did find a Mooney instructor to give me some better training in the airplane, especially with regard to power settings.

The Mooney had a 150hp engine, and would cruise almost 160 mph. I could make it to the Jersey shore, a popular destination, in less than an hour. I also used it on a number of business trips, especially down to the Fairchild Aircraft plant in

Hagerstown, MD, where we had some engineering and modification contracts.

On one such trip, I had taken along a non-pilot Air Force captain, and another civilian. The captain had no experience in light airplanes. On the way back, he got airsick, and used his hat for a sick-sack. He just threw the hat away and bought a new one. Word of this got back to the base, and for weeks, his fellow officers teased him with such remarks as, "Hey, Norm, nice hat. Is that new?"

Payments and upkeep got pretty burdensome, though, for all the use I was getting from the bird, so I sold a half share to a friend, who had just sold his Stinson. We got along very well for a few years until a devastating AD (airworthiness directive) came out on the wooden tail. Every year at annual inspection, the tail had to be dismantled and inspected for deterioration, and then reassembled. It was a very expensive procedure, so we decided to sell. We had to take a loss, because this AD also greatly decreased the value.

We finally located a buyer in New York City. My partner flew the airplane up to Middletown, NY, where the buyer had planned to store it, and I went up in a Cherokee to bring him back. When the guy showed up, he had all the money ($6,000) in cash. Apparently, he had gone to a number of banks and borrowed as much as he could without collateral at each one. Most of the money was in $50 bills, so we counted it out, and signed the airplane over to him. When we left, I stashed the money in the attaché I used as a flight case. We looked like a couple of drug dealers who had just made a big sale.

That was my last venture into ownership for some time. I had since moved to State College, and had several airplanes to fly there.

My first real airplane, the Aeronca Chief.

Ready to take off in my pride and joy.

The Ercoupe, both a joy to fly and a headache.

Chapter Three
The L-19

In a cost-cutting move in 1965, Secretary of Defense McNamara closed a number of military installations across the nation. The base where I worked was included among these, so I began to look for another job. On one trip for an interview, I ran into Penn State Professor Barney McCormick in the airline terminal. We knew each other casually, and he asked me where I was headed. When I told him where, he said, "Have you ever thought of going to grad school?"

That was, in fact, an option high on my list, and I told him so. He said, "Why don't you come up to Penn State and work for me? I have an Army research project to study trailing vortices, and we are doing experimental work with an L-19 they loaned us. I need someone to do research on this, to fly the airplane on the tests, and to do graduate work in conjunction. I can give you a full-time position as a research assistant."

It sounded like a position custom made for me. I couldn't believe they were going to pay me for this, although it was only about half of what I was making with the Air Force. I visited Penn State a few days later to work out the details, and moved to State College that September.

My checkout in the L-19, or Bird Dog, as it was known, was a little harried. I had trouble reaching the rudder pedals. I could actually touch them, but couldn't depress them all the way. We decided to try it anyway. On the first takeoff, I saw that this was a mistake. The L-19 had tremendous torque (or P-factor) and I couldn't keep it from running off to the side of the runway. In a last desperate attempt, I pulled back and nursed it off on the verge of a stall, as Barney yelled, "Not yet!"

I told him I had no choice, so after a successful landing, we went back to the ramp to look for a cushion. With none available, we found an old windsock, which we folded up into the shape of a cushion, and put behind me on the seat. It worked, and I made a much better second takeoff.

In test configuration, the L-19 had a big steel-tubing trusswork mounted behind the wing, and attached to the fuselage. A probe was attached to this support that spun in the rotating air of the vortex, and through instrumentation in the cabin, recorded the resulting rpm. It could be repositioned vertically in the air and moved spanwise by ground adjustment. We made scads of flights with this at various airspeeds, and with the probe in varying positions all through the wake behind the wing.

A second phase of the project was to measure the vortex farther downstream, which was done by flying past a ground-based array of sensors along the runway. To make sure the vortex was moving onto the sensor array, we had a 12ft-by-12ft steel frame supporting a wire mesh that had yarn tufts attached every few inches, which was placed between the sensor and the runway. As the pilot flew by, a signalman helped him get into position by signaling up or down, or right or left, with paddles like the old landing signal officer on an aircraft carrier.

This phase of the project came up in the summer of 1966. Unfortunately, Barney was scheduled to be away on a consulting job all summer, so I was appointed the acting project leader, and as the only pilot, had to do all the flying. We had a station wagon to carry the equipment and a crew of grad students working on the project. Every good-weather day, we would head to the airport, often in the evening, to get calm winds and set things up. The tuft grid was on a base with wheels, so we would tow it from the shed to the runway, and then set up the sensor array beside it with controls in the station wagon parked next to it. I would make continual circuits of the pattern and fly past the equipment until I got the vortex on the sensor and recorded enough data.

My part of the research project was to design modified wingtips in an attempt to reduce the strength of the trailing vortices. The test models were made of balsa wood and fiberglass, and were fabricated by the Engineering Shop. Once we had sufficient data for the standard configuration, we installed the modified tips, and then had to repeat all the tests for comparison.

The in-flight measurements with the probe on the aircraft still had to be done for the modified tips. We had initially planned this phase for the next summer, but in early 1967, the Army notified us that they wanted to have the L-19 back in a few months. It seems they had a little fracas going on in Southeast Asia, and needed it over there. We had a term break in early March, but the weather was far too unfavorable in Pennsylvania at that time of the year, so at the suggestion of the Army Research Office, located in Durham, NC, we planned to locate down there.

I flew the L-19 down with the test rack installed on the side of the fuselage, and Hal, my buddy and fellow grad student, went along as the crewman to operate the probe controls in the back. Barney flew down in the Department's Cherokee with Carl, his crewman. The L-19 was a bear to fly all that distance with the test rack installed. We actually took a break for coffee (and to rest my right foot) at Fredericksburg, VA.

Initially, we went into Raleigh-Durham Airport (RDU), but found it much too busy for our operations. As I was taxiing in there, I passed behind a DC-9 parked at the gate, and didn't realize the engines were being revved up. The wake caught my tail and spun me around almost 360 degrees. As I was in this merry-go-round ride, the tower said, "Army 274 (the tail number was 12274), caution, wake turbulence from that DC-9."

"Yes, we noticed that," I replied when I got straightened out.

We decided over lunch there that we would go over to Burlington, about fifty miles to the west. Burlington was an ideal airport. It was uncontrolled, but had quite adequate facilities. The FBO was very cooperative with our needs, and even offered use of their shop if we needed it, in true Southern-hospitality style.

We stayed in a Holiday Inn not far from the field, and each morning, we would head out to the airport for a planned set of tests. Hal and I would usually take off first with the probe in one spanwise position. He could then move it vertically in ¼-inch increments, and record the spinning RPM indicated at each point. A flight to make one complete vertical traverse took about an hour. When finished, we would land and move the probe an inch outboard. Barney and Carl would then go up and survey this position, while Hal and I would plot out our data and review it. We would keep alternating flights all day long, or until we were too tired to function effectively.

We made friends with some of the local aviators who hung out there. In particular, I remember one who, shall we say, did not exactly have a genius IQ. I never knew his correct name, but he worked part time at a print shop, so we called him simply "The Printer." One day, he was sitting there eating some kind of seeds from a brown paper bag. When we asked him what it was, he said, "Celery seed, for my cold."

I asked him if that helped a cold. He said, "I guess so. I went to the doctor, and he gave me this prescription. You know they write those in Latin, so I took it to the library and translated it, and it said 'celery seed.' So, instead of paying $20 or so at the drug store, I just went to the garden shop and bought fifty cents worth of celery seed."

He was a pilot, though, and flew the airport's Piper Cub occasionally. The grass beside the runway was used as a taxiway. One day when we had taxied out to the end, and were running up there, I saw this Cub approaching. As it got closer, it looked as if he was going to land on the grass. Then Hal said, "Watch out, it's the Printer!"

I gunned it and taxied out onto the runway as he passed right behind me. I never did know if he saw me, but we avoided a collision.

After about two weeks, we got all the data we needed, so we packed up and headed home. This time, I flew the Cherokee and Barney flew the L-19. On the way back, we were in a loose formation, and I observed Barney peeling off and descending. He appeared to be landing in a field, and I thought the engine had quit. I saw him taxiing, though, so I assumed it was something minor. I went on to Fredericksburg, where we had planned to land for lunch, and pretty soon, he came in. It turned out he had flown off the sectional chart, and couldn't find a Washington sectional. He spotted this farmer's field by a windsock on the barn, and landed, and the farmer gave him an old sectional. We made it home uneventfully after lunch.

The next trip in conjunction with the L-19 was actually in the Cherokee. Barney and I went to the Army Research Office in Durham to review the project and investigate the possibility of a follow-on. A stop at NASA Langley took all day, so we stayed overnight and met with the Army the next morning. Barney had flown down, so it was my turn to fly home.

I had checked the weather early in the morning, but not right before we left after lunch. It had been forecast to be clear all the way. I took off from Raleigh-Durham in the afternoon and headed north. After a short while, clouds started to develop. By the time we got into southern Virginia, they were solid and lowering, forcing me down to a few thousand feet. They kept lowering, and finally I was down below 1000 ft above the ground. I had no instrument training, so for the first time in my life, I seriously considered a precautionary landing in a field. I started to look for one when Barney said, "You better let me have it; I have a little instrument training."

I'm thinking he had five or ten hours. I was getting resigned to the fact that there was no way out of this. I was envisioning the typical accident report stating, "No mechanical or other causes for the fatal accident could be found."

Then it improved a little, and Barney turned it back over to me, since he had a little trouble seeing the instruments from the right seat. The airplane did have gyros, but only one little nav/com radio. Then, all of a sudden, the weather seemed to improve even more and we were in a big dome of clouds, with Dulles Airport in the middle of it. Apparently, the heat from this expanse of concrete was evaporating the moisture there.

I chopped the throttle, and tuned in Dulles Approach. "What are you going to do, land?" Barney said.

I thought that would be an obvious choice, but he seemed to think we were through the bad weather. After talking it over, we decided to land and check the weather closely at the Weather Bureau office there. It looked possible to continue, but it was very marginally VFR (visual flight rules), and we still had an hour to go. I opted to stay overnight. Barney was always very optimistic about making our intended flight, but I finally convinced him to stay. On the way into town (there were no motels around Dulles in those days), it started to rain. It rained all night and all the next day. Finally, when we awoke the second day there, it was starting to clear. We got to Harrisburg in the morning. By the time we got lunch there, it had cleared all the way to State College. That was probably my most harrowing trip ever.

In April, we got directions to return the L-19 (by then re-designated as an O-1) to the Cessna plant in Wichita. There, it would go through a full overhaul and some modifications, along with a number of other similar aircraft, and then be shipped over to Southeast Asia. I was designated to be the ferry pilot. It would be my longest cross-country trip to date. I had never flown on multiple legs with fuel stops, and stopping overnight, which was highly probable on this trip. The airplane was stripped of all test equipment and prepared for return.

My crewman, classmate and good buddy, Hal Sherrieb, and I ready to go on a vortex test run in the L-19.

In the L-19 cockpit in full gear.

The L-19 on a test flight with the probe-support rack

Chapter Four
Going Home

Wichita isn't nearly as far as Paris, and the route isn't over water, but, somehow, the flight that lay before me that chilly May morning seemed as daunting to me as the Lone Eagle's famous trek of forty years previous. In fact, it was almost forty years to the day.

My flight jacket felt good as I readied old Army 274 for the journey back to her place of birth. Preflighting the L-19 required some special techniques, like poking a wire up through the fuel drains to get the fuel to flow through the sludge. I also appreciated the Cessna engineer who put steps up the side of the fuselage, enabling one to visually check the fuel supply. If he were the same guy who designed the fuel gauges, I can understand his reasoning.

As I warmed up in the office, I went over the route on the charts. I had planned to make the first stop at Dayton, Ohio, and hoped to make St. Louis the first day. I gazed out at the L-19 and thought that it even bore somewhat of a resemblance to the Ryan NYP—high-wing, tail-dragger with an oversized engine, and drab looking with a strictly-business interior. But it wasn't just the appearance that led to the apprehension of this flight; it was the leaky primer that caused the engine to run rich, the balding tires, the weakening brakes, and a number of other items that had been decided to be left to the Army's overhaul program rather than to the dwindling funds of our research budget.

I donned my coveralls, stuffed a heavy cushion on the seat to replace the parachute that had been returned to the Army, and climbed aboard. The bird fired right up and climbed out briskly in the cool morning air. I thought of the contrast as Lindbergh sloshed through the wet grass at Roosevelt Field trying to nurse the overloaded Ryan into the air.

Within minutes, I was over unfamiliar territory in western Pennsylvania, and progressing slowly (90 knots minus headwind). Cross-country flying in the L-19 was somewhat demanding. It had no VOR (VHF omni range), only an ADF (automatic direction finder), but one of the best ADF's I have ever used. The only other radio was a seventeen-channel UHF com set, and, I might add, one of the worst I have ever used. It was crank-tuned with a "whistle-stop" receiver. You had to tune it slightly past the calibration signal, though, to get the receiver on the transmitter frequency.

The transmitter selector was calibrated in numbers from one to seventeen. The UHF frequencies had to be identified by reference to a chart, which I then had to refer to a second chart to tell me which UHF frequency goes with which facility. Only six of the seventeen channels actually worked, and the audio quality of these was about as good as that of an old four-channel Superhomer I had in my Ercoupe.

The gray blob that is marked on the chart as Pittsburgh came and passed below me (the mills were still operating then). As I got into Ohio, ground speed checks revealed a stronger headwind than anticipated, so it didn't look as if I would make Dayton. I decided that Columbus would be a safer bet.

About fifteen miles out, I tried to call Port Columbus tower on the "tower" channel (there was only one channel for all towers, just like my Superhomer). After several attempts with no success, I decided to land at Ohio State University Airport, which, at that time, had no tower. Approaching OSU, I realized I had been calling Port Columbus on the FSS frequency instead of the tower.

Oh, well, here I was approaching OSU, so I went on in. Here, I made the most beautiful three-point landing in all my hours in the airplane, and wouldn't you know, not a soul witnessed it. I landed on the back parallel runway, away from all the hangar/office buildings. I figured if I had jack-rabbited down the main runway, at least a dozen people would have seen me.

There was no restaurant then at OSU, and only sparse teletype weather info, so I made the short hop over to Dayton anyway. In those days, you could park on the lightplane ramp at the terminal, and fuel, food, and weather info was handily available. I went upstairs to the FSS and learned that a front was moving into the St. Louis area, but maybe, if I hurried, I could still beat it.

After a quick lunch, I took off and found a convenient highway to follow that went to Indianapolis, and then on to St. Louis. Navigation thus simplified, I began to crank around on the ADF to see if I could pick up anything useful. I ran across a continuous weather broadcast, which proved to be very fortunate. I learned that the front had already passed St. Louis, and was progressing toward Terre Haute.

Not only was this surprising, but also disappointing, because I was now picking up a slight tailwind, and hoped to go as far as I could with it. Another go around on the weather broadcast, however, convinced me that Indianapolis was as far as I would get that day.

I headed for Indianapolis International. In those days, I usually went into the major airports on long trips because I was unfamiliar with the area and unsure of the facilities at smaller ones. I called Indianapolis tower, this time on the correct frequency, and was advised, "Contact Indianapolis Approach this frequency."

Okay, "Indianapolis *Approach,* Army 274, 15 east for landing." I could swear it sounded like the same voice that responded and vectored me to the airport, and then turned me over to the tower again.

After landing, I was told to contact ground control, and not quite sure what to do, said, "Army 274 doesn't have ground control frequency." They responded, "Contact ground this frequency."

So, I punch the button again and say, "Indianapolis *Ground*, clear of active, like to proceed to parking." This time, I know it was the same voice that directed me to the ramp. It seemed funny to keep calling different controllers at a facility all on the same frequency, but that's the way it worked.

I taxied to the general aviation ramp, where I saw a big sign on the office that said "Turner." It was filled with Learjets, King Airs, twin Cessnas, and other fancy airplanes, so I parked my drab little bird on one of the back rows. I tied down and went inside to order fuel and inquire about lodging. As the attendant went to put in my fuel order, a large, impressive-looking man came down the stairs. He was graying in both his hair and moustache, but he looked strangely familiar—not like someone I knew, but someone I had seen in the movies or somewhere. He walked over to me, and said, "Are you being taken care of?"

"Yes, Sir," I replied, "they're just putting in my fuel order."

He then disappeared into a back room, and the attendant gave me directions to the Holiday Inn that was just across the street, and well within walking distance. Handy. I picked up my bag and started across. On the way, I passed the open hangar of the FBO, and noticed an old air racer hanging from the ceiling. How forlorn it looked, with fittings rusting, tires flat, and fabric cracking and peeling from the frame.

I gazed at it a bit, and then proceeded on. Then, suddenly, it hit me! Of course—the racer, Turner Aviation, a charismatic gentleman. That was Roscoe Turner! The famous race pilot of the 1930's was one of the most successful, and certainly the most flamboyant, race pilots of all time. He always wore a military-style uniform and traveled with his pet lion, Gilmore. I remembered reading that after retiring from racing, he opened an FBO at Indianapolis. Wow, I actually spoke to Roscoe Turner!

The motel was a very nice four-story facility, with a restaurant and cocktail lounge. After dinner, I relaxed in my room and heard it start to rain against the window. It rained all night and all the next day. I had to spend another night there.

That evening, I was sitting at the bar and struck up a conversation with a corporate pilot, also laying over there. When I told him of my two-night stay, he said, "Why couldn't you continue IFR?"

I told him that the L-19 wasn't equipped for IFR (instrument flight rules), with only an ADF for navigation. I didn't mention that I wasn't equipped for IFR, either. I didn't yet have an instrument rating.

The second morning there, I awoke to bright sunshine gleaming in through the drapes, and when I went to the window and opened them, I was greeted by a clear blue sky. Then, I looked across the parking lot to a flagpole, and was also greeted by a flag standing straight out. I was afraid that it pointed east. A call to flight service confirmed this. Indeed, the wind was directly out of the west, my exact intended heading. It was also very strong. I couldn't waste another night there, though, so I packed up and headed for the airplane, resigned to a long day's flight.

Handling the L-19 on the ground wasn't a piece of cake even on a calm day, and on a windy day, it was something else. It had taken me a while to get used to her quirky ground behavior, but once in the air, her rock-steady, beautiful air qualities made me fall in love with her. Like a woman, she could be exasperating at times, but these times were more than made up for by her moments of loving tenderness.

Somehow, I managed to get to the active runway and headed skyward. Skyward she went, too. In a wind like that, it seemed to climb faster than it moved forward. After climbing to a few thousand feet, I leveled off and took up my heading. Needless to say, it was rough! I had noticed on the chart that a major highway ran right by, and continued on to Kansas City. It made an excellent navigation aid.

After five minutes or so, I looked back and was surprised to see the airport was still practically under me. Then I looked down and saw the traffic on the highway outpacing me. I let down a thousand feet or so to gain some groundspeed. Then I noticed a little yellow Volkswagen Beetle catch up to me, pass me, and start to disappear in the distance. That was too much. I let down even farther, until I was only 1000 feet or a little less above the ground. Gradually, I caught up to the Bug and I passed him. Content with this minor victory, I relaxed and proceeded westward.

With all this wind, I knew my range calculations had to be pretty accurate. Also, my left fuel gauge had quit completely, so I had to go strictly on timing for fuel consumption. With about two hours fuel in each tank, I ran two hours on the left (the one with the bad gauge), and then switched. At this point, I was only about 100 miles from IND, so I began to look for a stop in about another 50 to 75 miles. Not much of a leg on a 1100-mile trip.

Not only did I need to locate a field within this range, but I had to find one with a runway headed west. I couldn't tolerate more than a few degrees of crosswind. I consulted the chart and saw that Vandalia, Illinois, fit this bill. I headed there, and on arrival, indeed found the wind to be right down the runway. Landing was not much of a problem, and I only used a small portion of the runway. The FBO was at the upwind end of the field, and I taxied there with little difficulty.

Taking off was different. There was no taxiway, so you had to back-taxi on the runway. When I rolled out onto it, I found this to be a daunting task. The wind was so strong that every time I let up on the brakes, the airplane would weathercock around into the wind. I would slowly work it around to head down the runway and inch ahead a few feet, but it would spin around again. As I slowly progressed down the runway, I looked up and saw a Cessna on final approach headed toward me. I couldn't alert him to my position because I only had UHF com, and I did not want to attempt pulling off into the grass. Hoping to avoid a "mid-ground," I called flight service.

"Vandalia radio, Army 274 is having a little (greatly understated) trouble taxiing, and, ah, unable to clear for landing traffic."

"Roger 274, the Skylane sees you. He's going around."

That was some relief. I continued to inch down the runway. Finally, I managed to get about 500 feet down the runway. I figured that, with this wind, I wouldn't need any more than that. It was almost as strong as my stall speed. I let it swing around one more time, and then opened the throttle. I lifted off with several hundred feet to spare. The Bird Dog went up like an elevator!

I picked up my concrete beacon again and proceeded westward. In another hour, I had crossed the Mississippi and assumed that I was now officially in (or over) the West. This time, I had pretty carefully planned this leg to Columbia, Mo. By the time I got there, the wind had died down a bit. It was only in the twenty-knot range, almost calm compared to what I had experienced on the previous leg. Landing was relatively easy, a welcome change.

I refueled and got lunch at the small restaurant there. I also saw a case containing hoagies, prepared to go. I got one of these, just in case I would have to land somewhere later that had no food facilities. I stuffed it into the map case and fired up again for my westward trek.

Flight Service handled traffic advisories there, so I gave them a call. Apparently, they must have had frequent National Guard visitors, because they asked, "Army 274, is this a round robin?"

Boy, there was a straight line begging for a clever reply, but I tried to suppress the urge and remain professional. "Negative, 274 is on a ferry flight to Wichita."

This was my last transmission on the FSS frequency, because that channel went out shortly after departing Columbia. The right fuel gauge also became highly inaccurate about this time. The wind was subsiding, though, and the decreased headwind and turbulence began to make the flight enjoyable again. My affection for the old girl was returning.

I was doing very careful, almost constant, speed checks, flying with stick in the right hand, and the E6B computer in the left. As I neared Kansas City, I found my groundspeed had picked up considerably. I had originally thought I may have to land somewhere in that area, but now I thought I could make it all the way to Wichita. At KC, I turned to the southwest, and actually picked up a slight tailwind. What a change!

At this point, I departed the highway, however, and found the terrain through this part of Kansas to be very sparse. There were no roads to follow, no towns, and hardly even any buildings. Navigation was getting to be a real challenge, since I had no opportunity to have established a heading. Then I noticed a beacon right on the airport at Wichita. I cranked the ADF around until I picked it up, and found a strong signal. The needle swung around to zero, and I homed in on this facility.

In a few minutes, the shores of my make-believe Europe were in sight. I flew right smack over Paris, er, Wichita, and called the tower. Whada-ya-know, the tower frequency still worked. As I approached the field as triumphant as Lindbergh arriving at Orly, in my head I could see the crowds converging and cheering, "He's made it! He's made it!"

In reality, though, there was no fanfare. It was Saturday evening, and the airport was very quiet. By the time I landed, the wind was picking up again, but this time, out of the north. That accounted for the tailwind I had had. My last landing in the old bird was a little sloppy. I had gotten a bit complacent after fighting the strong winds all day.

Once on the ground, I asked for the way to the Cessna plant and was directed to a small taxiway off one of the regular taxiways that wound over to it. As I approached the Cessna ramp, I had forgotten that the wind was pretty strong again, and all of a sudden I ground-looped almost 360 degrees. The only damage was to my pride. This was the only time I let the airplane get the best of me, and it was during the last two minutes I would be in it. Darn. Perhaps it was the old gal's way of chastising me for neglecting her momentarily as I basked in my own sense of accomplishment.

Oh, well, I had completed the trip flawlessly otherwise, so I proceeded to taxi onto the ramp. I saw a long row of the L-19's siblings along the edge of the ramp, so I taxied to the first open space in the line, swung around beside the others, and shut down. My L-19 adventures were over.

I gathered up my belongings and headed across the deserted ramp. I found a lone attendant inside one office, and he seemed to know exactly what to do as far as paperwork was concerned. He filled out a form, which I signed, and gave me a copy. The airplane was now officially back in Army hands. He also directed me to a small motel just in front of the airport. I checked in and then booked an airline flight back home the next day. (In those days you could do that.)

Early the next morning, as we climbed out in one of those weird-colored Braniff 727's, I looked over and saw old Army 274 tied down in the warm spring sun. I bade her a fond and somewhat sad farewell. Then, suddenly, a thought hit me—the hoagie! I had left the hoagie in the map case to sit there for who knows how long until they roll her in for maintenance. Oh, well, maybe it was retribution for her slapping me at the last moment for just a few seconds of neglect.

As we bored up toward the flight levels, I leaned back in my seat…and I smiled.

Chapter Five

Flight Testing

When I completed my master's degree in December 1968, the Department Head called me in and offered me a position on the regular faculty. I had been teaching a number of courses during my graduate work, and they needed another faculty in the area that I taught. It was the lowest paying offer I received, but I realized that it was a rare opportunity. I accepted, and was promoted to assistant professor.

One of the courses that I had become particularly involved in was the course in flight test engineering. This course involved an in-flight lab, where we took the students up in groups of three to measure the aircraft's performance. It was our reason (excuse) for owning an airplane. We performed experiments to determine the drag, stall speed, cruise speed, rate-of-climb, takeoff distance, and several other parameters. The practice was to have this course taught by a faculty member who was also a pilot, so that he could fly the labs as well as give the lectures. It was a natural for me.

The lab was initially conducted on Saturday mornings so as not to interfere with normal class schedules. The first group would meet at the airport at 8:00, and it would take about an hour for the experiment. By the time we got back, the 9:00 group would be there, and so on. We conducted this course for about thirty years without any mishaps. There were, however, a number of interesting incidents with students.

One year, there was a student named Faust in one of the groups. He was in the right front seat during the one experiment, and on takeoff, the door popped open. He jumped and grabbed onto the seat. His buddies in back, sensing his plight, sympathetically yelled, "Hey, Faust, if you fall out, can we have your Triumph?"

Of course, there was no danger. A cracked door just makes a lot of wind and noise. I went around and landed, closed the door, and continued on with the flight.

Another group one year was a little gung-ho. They wanted to do something daring in the airplane. They kept asking, "Prof. Smith, can we do some stunts?"

I tried to convince them that the Cherokee was not built for aerobatic maneuvers, and I shouldn't do extreme maneuvers with students, anyway. That did not seem to satisfy them because they just kept needling me on each flight. Finally, one day, I said, "Okay, we'll do a wing-over."

This is not an extreme maneuver, although I may have exceeded the limit pitch angle for a normal category airplane a bit. I put it into a dive, increased power, and pulled up sharply, then chopped the throttle. Just before stall, I kicked hard right rudder, and we went weightless as we yawed around 180 degrees. In the middle of this action, I heard a voice from the rear seat slowly and deliberately say, "Oh…my…God!"

I let the nose drop pretty steeply to regain speed, and then gradually leveled off. I said, "Do you want to do another one?"

"No, no, no, that's okay," was the reply. I never heard another peep out of them about doing "stunts."

The most memorable incident in this course occurred, though, not in flight, but in class. In the beginning of the course, I arranged the lab groups and wrote out the schedule on the blackboard. After we got everybody placed in an appropriate time slot, I would list the weight of each student next to the name. Then we would total these for each group. This practice served to simplify the calculation of weight and balance, and also insured that a group was not too heavy that the gross weight limit was exceeded.

I usually had all males in this class, but one year there was one female. When I came to her name, I said, "I'm sorry, Mary, but I have to ask you your weight."

She gave me some figure, which I listed, and then proceeded on to the next student. After a while, she raised her hand, and when I responded, she said, "Prof. Smith, I gave you my weight with no clothes on."

Without thinking, I quickly replied, "Well, that's okay if that's how you plan to fly."

The class roared—all except her. She glared at me and came up after class and said, "I didn't think that remark was very funny."

I tried to assure her that I didn't mean anything by it, and was merely trying to inject a little humor into the class. This was around 1970, an era when social causes were in the forefront. Women's lib, of course, was one of these. I was not used to such sensitivity, but, after that, I was very careful what I said when there were women in the class.

When I took over this course, we had a Piper Cherokee 180, and we used the standard instruments in the aircraft to measure the various flight parameters. A few years later, we acquired a Piper Arrow, which allowed for a wider range of tests. We could measure much of the performance, such as drag, rate-of-climb and descent, etc., in both the gear-up and gear-down configurations. Piper Aircraft also gave us their old airspeed boom and sensitive airspeed indicator, which enabled much more accurate measurements and a more realistic test scenario for the students.

The course became very popular and served as a model for a number of other universities who were considering similar courses. After ten or fifteen years, however, the fun of flying as part of my job wore off. Dragging out to the airport to prep the airplane at 0700 two or three times a week got to be a real chore. We acquired several graduate students over the years who were experienced pilots or flight instructors, so I was quite happy to turn much of the flying part of the course over to them.

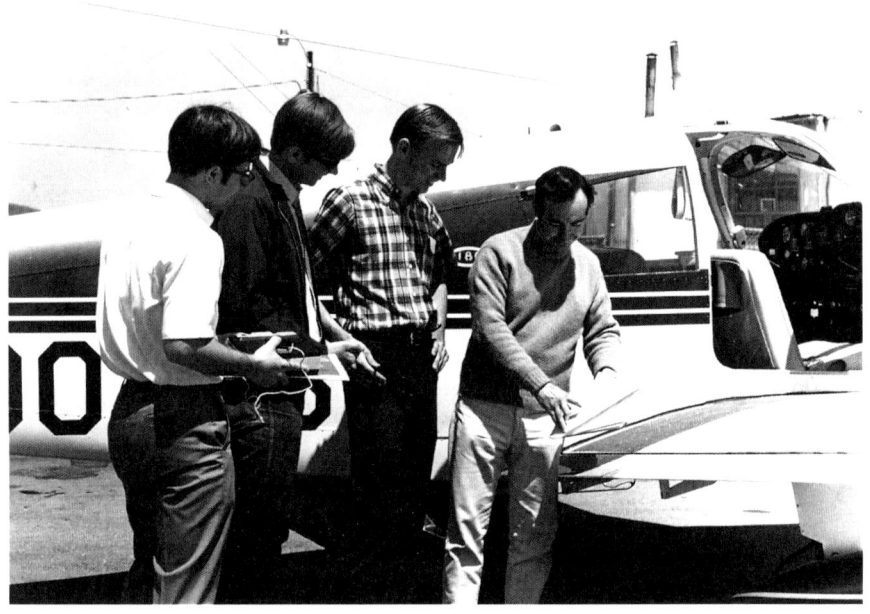

Briefing a student group prior to a flight test lab experiment.

The Piper Arrow, our later test aircraft, with airspeed boom modification.

Chapter Six
Air Pollution

There was an interdisciplinary research group on campus in the 1960's known as the Air Environment Center. The group did research on environmental issues, as the name implies, and consisted of faculty from meteorology, chemistry, biology, and a few other disciplines. One of the grants they had was to study the dispersion of air pollution downwind of a polluting source. By 1970, they had developed a mathematical model for this process, and were ready to run experiments to test it. This part of the project required an airplane, so they worked out an arrangement to use ours.

The back seat of the Cherokee was removed, and a large aluminum plate installed all the way through the baggage area, to which test equipment could be attached. A side-facing jump seat was installed for the equipment operator. A probe was attached under the right wing, essentially a scoop, to run air through a hose into the analyzing equipment.

A group of advanced grad students from meteorology, led by one of them, Dennis Trout, made up the research team. Dennis and two students planned to drive to the test site in a station wagon, also rigged up with test equipment, to make ground measurements. Another grad student, Stan, was to be the operator in the airplane. I was designated as the pilot for this operation. The team had selected East St. Louis, Ill. as the pollution source, an area of numerous chemical plants. They left it to me to select the airport. A quick look at the chart revealed Bi-State Airport, right in East St. Louis, to be the obvious choice.

Dennis and crew headed out in the station wagon, and Stan was to fly with me. After the ground crew was in position, we took off one morning, made a fuel/lunch stop in Dayton, and then headed for Bi-State. It was a beautiful VFR day, but as we neared our destination, the air got hazier. The closer we got, the hazier it got. I was having trouble finding the airport, so I tuned in the ADF to the beacon on the field. I could see the ground right below, but not at any appreciable slant distance. As I was staring down over the side, my peripheral vision caught the ADF needle swing around suddenly. I banked steeply, and there was the airport right below. I spiraled down, keeping the field in sight all the time, and found the haze to improve a lot at pattern altitude. I made a normal VFR approach and landing.

Bi-State was an ideal airport for us. There was no tower, but it was pretty active, and had good facilities. Parks College operated their flight activities there. The FBO was also very friendly, and gave us a parking spot right outside the office, near to a gate, where we could bring the station wagon in.

Dennis and his crew had obtained lodging somewhere to the east of town, and I had made reservations for Stan and me at a nearby Holiday Inn. We rented a car and drove over there. I was somewhat surprised to find a gated chain-link fence surrounding the motel, with a sign by the gate that said, "Locked after 10:00 P.M. For admittance, buzz the office, and provide identification."

It was right in the middle of the industrial city, so it seemed somewhat logical. We turned in early, and I kept hearing sirens much of the night. I figured that we were near a firehouse or police station. In the morning, when we went to breakfast, I picked up a local paper and was greeted by the headline, "Riots intensify again!"

Well, that explained the sirens, the fence, and the locked gate. It was 1970, an era of racial and anti-war demonstrations around over the country. Apparently, the town was plagued by a series of race riots for several months. I learned much later that East St. Louis was referred to as the Harlem of the St. Louis area.

We had no real trouble, though, and were too busy to pay much attention to the local activity. Early each morning, we would drive over to the airport, and the rest of the crew would meet us in the station wagon, hook up the probe, and adjust the equipment for the day's experiments. I would wait inside the office and have a cup of coffee while studying the planned route on the chart. This was not an unpleasant place to wait because the young lady who attended the desk was gorgeous. She always wore a miniskirt, the latest fashion craze, and could easily have passed for a *Playboy* model.

One morning, as I was sipping my coffee, she came around the end of the counter and passed by me to go outside. She had on an especially short miniskirt that day. Just then, a flight instructor came to the door and said, "Hey, Jennifer, will you get me a St. Louis chart?"

Instead of going back and around the counter, she just leaned over it to retrieve the chart from behind—way over. Wow! I wasn't prepared for such a sight that early in the morning. She got it and went on outside. Right then, my crew came in and said, "Hey, Skip, we're ready to fly."

I was too shook up to fly right at that moment. I don't think I could have even remembered the starting procedure. "Just give me a minute to finish my coffee," I said.

Pretty soon, I regained my composure and went out to climb into the cockpit. Each day, we would fly a route that roughly approximated a radial out from the city. At an appointed checkpoint, Dennis's crew would take a measurement on the ground and we would circle overhead and take measurements at 500 feet, then at 1000, and so on up to a few thousand. We had a waiver from the FAA to fly at 500 feet over the congested area. Then, we would go out a few miles and repeat the procedure. We could get about two different routes measured in a day.

By the end of the day on Thursday of that week, Dennis concluded that we had sufficient data, so we packed up to go home on Friday. Stan and I took off right after lunch. The weather was reported to be pretty bad farther east, and even IFR within about fifty miles of our location. I filed IFR to Indianapolis, a fairly short trip, and planned to check there for conditions farther east. I had just recently gotten my instrument rating, so I didn't want to push it too hard.

I was skimming the clouds within twenty or thirty miles, and in them from about fifty miles on. I made a successful ILS (instrument landing system) into Indianapolis, though, my first real one, and taxied into the now somewhat familiar Turner ramp. I went into the office and called flight service. I informed them of my intended flight to State College, if not that day, perhaps the next one.

"How about next Tuesday?" the briefer said, and then hastened to add, "I'm not kidding. It's snowing there now. There's a big low pressure area over Pennsylvania, and not expected to move out until early next week."

I gave Stan the bad news, and he said, "Oh, man, I have a big exam on Tuesday, and have to get home to study for it. Do you mind if I take a bus?"

I told him not at all. I preferred to be alone on layovers. That way, I can set my own schedule and not be pressured to push weather to get home. He got his bag and headed for the bus station. I grabbed mine and headed over for the Holiday Inn.

As I was getting on the elevator to go to my room, a USAir crew got on the same elevator. I heard the stewardesses (they were still called that then) talking about something that occurred in Philadelphia that morning. "Did you just come from Pennsylvania?" I asked the captain.

When he replied affirmatively, I asked him how the weather was back there and told him of my intended route in a Cherokee. "Forget it," he said, laughing, "we just barely made it out of there in our DC-9."

Well, that confirmed the report from flight service. I settled in and prepared for a long weekend in Indianapolis.

Roscoe Turner had died since my last visit, and I learned that they had erected a museum in his honor right next to the FBO. I went over there on Saturday. It was not a large museum, but nicely laid out. Right in the middle of the floor was the Turner racer, all cleaned up and restored. I was glad to see it rescued from its inglorious perch under the ceiling of the hangar.

On the right of the racer was Turner's Packard sedan, also restored to mint condition. On the other side was Gilmore, the lion. It was really him, stuffed and mounted in a lifelike pose. Around the sides of the museum were cases of trophies and other memorabilia. Above them were scads of pictures and descriptions of Roscoe's various exploits. I figured that the average person would spend about twenty or thirty minutes looking over this stuff. For an aviation history buff like me, though, it took several hours. I carefully studied each display, and read the descriptions. After all, I had a vested interest in this man. I had met him!

In the evenings, I would relax around the piano bar in the lounge. A middle-aged woman played and sang there each night. I had made friends with some of the locals, particularly the local postmaster. He related all sorts of intimate details to me about the singer. I didn't really think he had any way of knowing these things, but they made a good story. At her breaks, the entertainer would often join an older man at his table. "Who is that guy?" I asked the postmaster. "Is that her husband, or what?"

"That's her sugar daddy," he replied. "He takes care of her...and she takes care of him, if you know what I mean." I knew what he meant.

Each day, I would check the weather with flight service. Finally, on Monday morning, they informed me that the weather was VFR through Ohio, and was expected to clear up through Pennsylvania later in the day. I checked out and headed for the airplane.

I was a little overconfident and set out VFR. By the time I got south of Dayton, the clouds were building up. I started to climb, and it was a contest between the clouds and me to see who could ascend faster. When I saw them outpacing me, I headed for a little valley between the storms and nursed the Cherokee upward as fast as I could get it to go. I should have been alarmed, but instead, I felt exhilarated. I was in a duel with nature. I related to the scene in *Patton*, where he led his troops into his first battle, and with bullets flying and shells exploding all around him, he exclaims, "God, how I love it!"

Like Patton, I won my battle against nature (barely), and headed on to Columbus. There, I filed IFR the rest of the way home, and had an uneventful flight.

A few weeks later, the Air Environment Center had analyzed the data from our flights and decided that additional tests would be helpful. They wanted to go out to East St. Louis again and expand the study. Win Philips, a newly licensed pilot on our faculty, was anxious to build up flying time, so he volunteered to fly this phase. I gladly relinquished the reins.

A few days after he departed, however, he called me on his way back, and said that he had hit bad weather and needed to get home for other obligations. He wondered, if he abandoned the airplane and took an airliner, if I could retrieve it. Ironically, he was in Indianapolis!

A few days after that, I was on an airliner headed to Indianapolis. I got to spend one more night in the famous motel. The next morning, I called a friend who was on the faculty of the Aviation Department at Ohio State and asked if he could meet me for lunch. It would be convenient because his office was on the OSU airport. He happily agreed, so I headed for Columbus.

As I was taxiing in, the tower asked, "Have you shot anyone down with that rocket launcher under your wing?"

"That's a probe," I replied. "We're from Penn State doing some air pollution research."

"Oh, welcome aboard, Penn State," the tower replied cheerfully, and they ushered me to a prime parking spot at the front of the ramp.

Stacy and I had a nice lunch, catching up on recent activities, and then I taxied out to depart for home. I made the usual call to the tower. "OSU tower, Cherokee nine zero seven papa Sierra, ready for takeoff."

The tower responded, "Nine zero seven Penn State, cleared for takeoff. Have a nice flight."

"Roger, OSU, thanks for your hospitality."

I loved such camaraderie. I get the same warm feeling when I'm driving my vintage Corvette, and if I pass another Corvette, we wave to each other.

Chapter Seven
Agnes

Every June, the American Society for Engineering Education (ASEE) holds a national conference, usually at some university willing to host it. In 1972, it was at Texas Tech in Lubbock, and I had a paper accepted for presentation there. Barney and Win also had business at this conference, so it was decided that we would fly out in the Cherokee. We also took along a professor from mechanical engineering as a passenger.

Fortunately, on the Saturday we departed, the weather was beautiful all across the country. I flew the first leg to Dayton, then Win took us on to St. Louis, and Barney flew from there to Tulsa, where we stopped for the night. The next morning, it looked like we could make it non-stop to Lubbock, and Win, still trying to log time, volunteered for this leg. I rode right seat and helped with the navigation. We had no DME (distance measuring equipment), and this was long before GPS, so one of the main duties of the right-seater was to determine groundspeed by timing the passage of landmarks and updating the range.

It was a long leg, and we had a slight headwind, so I suggested that we might want to make an intermediate fuel stop. Win agreed, and we noted Childress, TX, was right along our route, so it was a logical stop. It appeared to be a fair-sized airport, with three runways. When we got there, however, we found that only one was useable. The other two were closed, and crumbling, with grass growing up through the cracks. It was sort of a rundown field.

We taxied to the only FBO and parked in front of what appeared to be the maintenance hangar. The door was open, and a Cessna was inside with the cowling off, and tools strewn around on the floor beneath it. A loud radio was blaring country music in the background, but we couldn't find anyone around. We yelled and went on into the office, but it, too, was vacant. Then, we spotted the flight service station some distance away, so we hiked over to it and found a lone attendant, apparently the only soul on the airport.

We asked him if anybody attended the FBO, and he said, "Yeah, Jake ought to be over there." Then he looked at the clock, and added, "Oh, but it's almost noon, so he probably went to lunch…and it's Sunday, so he won't be back until after two o'clock."

We couldn't wait that long. We checked the winds pretty carefully and decided to try to make Lubbock. I diligently kept calculating groundspeed and determined that we could make it, but with only a small reserve of fuel. We did.

The trip out had been in all-beautiful VFR weather, but the return was a different story. Barney had wanted to be dropped off in Dallas to do some consulting work on the return trip on Thursday. My old grad school buddy, Hal, lived and worked in Dallas, so I called him and asked if we could touch base on this visit. He informed me that Jim, another fellow grad student who lived in Ft. Worth, would be there for dinner on Wednesday, along with their wives, and suggested that I come over Wednesday and join them, then stay overnight. Sounded like a good plan. My meetings all ended on Tuesday. I caught an American Convair for Dallas on Wednesday.

One adjustment in the plan was that I would stay with Jim and his wife in Ft. Worth, because they had better guest facilities. I made arrangements for Barney to pick me up at Oak Grove Airport, just south of Ft. Worth. Jim's wife ran me down there early Thursday morning to await the arrival of the Cherokee around noon. We had planned to go over to Redbird Field in Dallas for lunch, drop Barney, and then Win and I would continue on toward home.

Noontime came and went, however, and no sign of the Cherokee. I ate some snacks from the vending machines, the only source of food there. I waited some more, and read every magazine in the pilot lounge. Finally, a little after four o'clock, Barney arrived. Win had injured his back playing tennis, so another M.E. professor gave Win his airline ticket in exchange for a seat on the Cherokee. I was now the only pilot from Dallas on.

Instead of lunch, we had dinner in Dallas, and we didn't get off until after 6:00—to head for Pennsylvania. It was a long flight across east Texas, and by the time we got into Arkansas, it was getting dark. I suggested that we stop overnight at Little Rock, and my passengers readily agreed. It had been a long day.

By the time we got to Little Rock, it was dark. It had been some time since I had made a night landing, and I probably wasn't current, but I got us down safely. We got a taxi to a nearby motel and went right to bed.

The next day when we went to breakfast, one of the guys said that he had heard something on TV about a hurricane in Pennsylvania. "A hurricane? In Pennsylvania?" I asked. "It couldn't be much of a hurricane there. Probably just the remnants of one going up the coast." Wrong!

I planned the first leg of the day to Nashville, and it was good weather all along that route. We taxied up in front of the flight service station at Nashville and I went in to check the weather the rest of the way. I was greeted by a big red hurricane symbol on the map behind the desk, and it was right over Pennsylvania! *Hmm*, I thought, *maybe there is something to this hurricane after all.*

"Can I help you?" the briefer asked.

"Well, I don't know," I said, "I'm trying to get to State College, Pa., right in the middle of that hurricane symbol I see."

"Oh, you won't get there," he said. "Hurricane Agnes is devastating Pennsylvania. There are extensive floods, most of the airports are closed, and we only have sketchy information from the few points that are reporting."

I gave the guys the bad news. We decided to continue on as far as we could, which looked like Cincinnati. The clouds were backed up through most of Ohio. I planned Louisville as an alternate if we couldn't make Cincinnati. Close to Louisville, I called flight service, and learned that Greater Cincinnati (now Cincinnati Northern Kentucky Intl.), southwest of town, was marginal VFR, but Lunken, on the east side, was totally socked in. The main airport was a better choice, anyway, because there was a motel right on the field. I had stayed there on a previous airline trip. We made it in there okay.

The next morning, it was IFR there, and all the way home. The brunt of the storm, however, had moved off the coast, and all that remained were lingering, but thick, clouds. I studied the situation carefully, and said, "Okay, guys, here's the story: We have about a 50-50 chance of getting into University Park, but I don't have enough fuel to go from here, try an approach, and then go to an alternate airport if I have to. So, we'll go to Columbus and refuel, and then I'll have plenty of range to try alternate plans."

I filed IFR, and we departed. Of course, we were in the clouds shortly after liftoff. Now, all the previous flights that my passengers had experienced on this trip were in beautiful weather. This was their first time in the clouds, and they are looking out at the same view that I had: nothing! I sensed their anxiety, but I was too busy flying the airplane to allay their fears.

We went into Port Columbus, and it was pretty busy with airline traffic, so approach control was vectoring me all around to mesh me in with it. After numerous heading changes, I finally got vectored to the localizer, and cleared for the ILS. It was no sweat, and we broke out at about 700 or 800 feet, and right on the centerline. After I landed, one of the guys said, "We were surprised that we broke out headed right down the runway."

"Well, yeah, that's sorta the way it's supposed to work," I told them.

I learned much later that they had assumed that all the heading changes I was being given were corrections to get me back on course after I screwed up. When I went into flight service to get a weather update, they headed down the hall. When they came back, they said, "We rented a car, and we're going to drive home from here."

Apparently, they had had enough of flying in the clouds, and the perceived ineptness of the pilot. Once on my own, I decided to stay over another day, since the weather was improving slightly each day. There was a Sheraton right on the airport, and within walking distance. So, bag in hand, I hiked over there. It was a very nice motel with a restaurant and comfortable rooms.

Since it was still morning, I went over to the airline terminal. I browsed the shops, had some lunch, and picked up some snacks and magazines. Then I settled in for a relaxing afternoon in my room. It was a nice respite in the midst of this challenging trip. I watched an old Errol Flynn movie, where, in one of his famous swashbuckling roles, he played a knight in love with the queen, and he would climb up the castle walls for rendezvous in her chambers. It's funny how I remember what movies I watched when weathered in somewhere.

In the evening, I went down to the dining room for dinner. There were two couples sitting at the next table, and the one guy kept looking over at me. Finally, he came over and said, "Aren't you from Harrisburg?"

"I used to be; I live in State College now," I replied.

"I thought so," he went on, "I used to see you around the Harrisburg airport."

It turned out that he and his partner were pilots for Hershey Foods. They had brought the company's Sabreliner out there to escape the storm (there was concern of the airport flooding), and along with their wives, were waiting it out. This was a fortunate coincidence. They had a pilot contact back in Harrisburg, who gave them inside info on the weather, and the status of the airport. It was actually useable, although officially listed as closed.

The next morning, armed with this information, and a careful look at the FSS reports, I decided to set out for home. The weather was reported for University Park, and hovered right around minimums, but airports to the south were open, and Harrisburg was now possible. I filed IFR, took down a clearance on the ramp, and taxied to the assigned runway. I carefully went through my IFR checklist. The last item on the list was "pencil." I had to have a pencil to copy down frequency changes and clearance amendments.

"Pencil?" I didn't seem to have a pencil. I knew I had one, because I had copied the clearance. I looked all around. Finally, in desperation, I pulled on the parking brake, unbuckled my harness, rolled back the seat, and climbed down on the floor to search. After looking all around, I spotted it way back along the seat track, but I couldn't seem to reach it.

About this time, I realized I had been down there a while, so I raised up to look out the window to check if everything was okay. I spotted two other airplanes waiting for takeoff beside me, but I was number one. I went back down, and with a maximum stretch, finally retrieved the pencil. I quickly climbed back into the seat, buckled in, and announced to the tower that I was ready for takeoff.

After I leveled off at my assigned altitude and adjusted power for cruise, I started to think about what must have been going through the minds of those pilots on the taxiway behind me. They had pulled up at the end of the runway, looked over, and saw an airplane with engine running, but apparently nobody inside it. Then, a head pops up at the window, and then disappears again. I had a good laugh at myself for my unorthodox behavior, and it relaxed me for the flight.

When I arrived at the Philipsburg VOR (VHF omni range, navigation beacon), the initial approach fix for UNV (University Park), I was given a hold at 7,000 feet. There were other aircraft holding below me. One by one we were stepped down to 4,000, and cleared for the approach. It's seven and a half miles over several mountain ranges from the VOR to UNV. As I let down, I kept looking for the ground, but all I could see was cloud. Finally, I got to minimum altitude and caught a few glimpses of the ground through some holes, but the clouds seemed to extend well below me. There was a DME step-down point past the last ridge, but I didn't have DME.

Then, I came to a slightly larger hole and saw a trailer court below. It had to be Continental Courts, the only trailer court anywhere along this route, and I knew it was the location of the

DME fix. What better indication of your position could you have than a visible landmark on the ground? I let down a few hundred feet more, and I broke out. I later used this method again, and called it my Continental Courts approach.

The airport appeared a few miles ahead, but what really startled me was the water. There was water everywhere! What I remembered as farm fields were now lakes. The airport looked high and dry, however, so I let down to traffic pattern altitude, and set up a downwind leg for runway 24. As I taxied in, I saw a number of military vehicles and personnel on the ramp. When I parked, a Civil Air Patrol cadet came out with a clipboard and asked me questions about my flight. They were interviewing pilots to better determine weather and airport conditions around the area. Apparently, this was one of the few airports open in the area, and they were using it for emergency operations.

State College had only minor effects from the rain, with just flooded basements and some low areas of streets. Fortunately, I lived in a second floor apartment at the time. I was very glad to be home, but I also felt a little let down. The challenge that Agnes had presented to me over the past few days was now gone, and this adventure was over.

Chapter Eight
Turbulence

Later that summer, after Agnes subsided, I got involved in another project. There was a group of professors in our department who did research on turbulence in fluids. They had a grant to develop a theoretical model for predicting the behavior of turbulence in the atmosphere, under certain atmospheric conditions. They had just completed the first attempt at this task, and were now ready to test it with in-flight measurements.

Once again, the Cherokee was pressed into service. The rear seat was removed, and the floor plate was installed. Special equipment was mounted there to detect the signals from a hot-wire probe mounted in the wingtip, and operated from a jump seat, as had been done on the air pollution project.

A Japanese grad student known as Kuni (short for a much longer full name) was in charge of this phase of the project, and Ed Jordan, the department electronic technician, was the operator to occupy the jump seat. He was quite experienced with both making and using hot-wire probes. Once again, I was designated as the pilot.

The study required flat, open terrain, with wind and/or thermal-generating warm weather; they left it up to me to pick an appropriate site. Since I had just returned from Texas, I remembered the area south and west of Dallas as meeting the criteria, and Red Bird Field seemed like a good base from which to operate. The team bought my choice.

Ed headed out in a station wagon containing a lot of tools and test equipment, while Kuni was scheduled to fly down with me. He had some flying experience, so he could assist me occasionally from the right seat. He was a friend, and a very likeable and witty guy. Once, when fire trucks were racing past our office with sirens blasting, he remarked that it reminded him of World War II. I agreed, and we started relating our childhood memories of the war. Then he added, "Like the damn B-29's coming again!" I then realized our memories of WWII were quite different.

The meteorology department at PSU had a weather observation tower on top of the building in which they were located, and I frequently went over there to look over the situation before a flight. They had maps and reports from all over the country; often, a meteorology professor who would assist me would be there. The day before our Texas run, I went up there and fortunately ran into Prof. John Cahir, one of their best weather interpreters. After I told him of our intentions, he took a look at things. He then turned to me, and said, "See this front hanging across the upper mid-west? Before you go tomorrow, check where it is then. If it is in the same place, it should stay there all day, so go south of it. But, if it has started to move, it will move south fast, so go above it."

Early the next morning, I called flight service and got an accurate location of the front. It was still in the same place. We'll go south!

We headed for Lexington, KY, on the first leg, where we got fuel and lunch. By the time we were ready to go again, it was almost the middle of the afternoon, so we made a short hop to Nashville and packed it in for the night. The next morning, I went into the flight service station, hoping not to see any hurricane symbols this time. When I informed the briefer we were headed for Dallas, he looked at things, and said, "It should be VFR all the way to Dallas, but, if you want to get out of here VFR, you better be quick. There's a front moving in pretty fast from the north."

Aha, the front John warned me about was on the move. Kuni and I hurried out to the airplane, but halfway across the ramp, it started to rain. We turned and ran back into flight service. The briefer was standing there watching us, and said, "I told you you had to be quick."

I replanned the flight and filed IFR to Muscle Shoals, AL, pretty much southward, hoping to outrun the front. The plan worked; about 75 miles south, we ran out of the clouds and into beautiful blue skies. I cancelled IFR and turned more to the west. For some reason, I distinctly remember tooling along on that leg, and thinking to myself that this actual flight didn't seem a whole lot different from the way I imagined it in the fantasy flights I had made as a boy in my PS-1 mock-up.

We landed at Greenwood, MS, and when we got out of the airplane, it was like climbing into an oven. There was a real heat wave, and the temperature was about 100 degrees. This was Kuni's first visit to Mississippi, and he always remembered it as the hottest place in the country. We had to make one more fuel stop at Texarkana, and then flew non-stop to Dallas. We had called Ed to give him an ETA, and he met us at Redbird Field with the station wagon.

The next morning, Kuni and Ed installed the probe and adjusted the equipment, and we set out for a test hop. When I lifted off, the airplane felt really funny. The pitch control was very light, and not very responsive. I figured that this was what test pilots meant when they described an airplane as feeling "squirrely." I managed to get it under control, however, and, after flying a while, got sort of used to the new feel. I suspected a CG (center of gravity) problem.

When we got back, I asked the guys if they had given me the correct weights and locations of the various pieces of equipment on the diagram they had supplied me. I had used it to carefully calculate CG range. "Oh, we added a few pieces after that was made up," I was told, "and we had to install some fairly heavy batteries for one item."

Well, that explained it, but it was too late to do anything about it out here in the field. I had to get used to flying the airplane like that. When we got home, I had it weighed with all equipment installed, and found the loaded CG way past the aft limit—almost to the point of neutral stability.

Each morning, following my usual custom, I would wait in the office while the rest of the crew installed the probe and made adjustments to the equipment. One morning, I watched a Learjet being towed up from the hangar area by a tug. It was driven by a teenage boy, who parked the Lear on the ramp right outside, then disconnected the tug and came into the office. After a few minutes, the manager said, "Here comes the colonel!"

The kid jumped up and ran outside to meet a shiny Cadillac pulling up by the jet. A large, distinguished-looking man got out and climbed aboard, as the kid took out his baggage from the trunk and stowed it in the airplane's baggage compartment. Then he closed up the jet and drove the car down to the hangar area. "Who is that guy with the Learjet?" I casually asked the manager.

"Oh, he's not the owner," he replied, "he's just the pilot."

I learned that the airplane belonged to the owner of a large department store in Dallas, and his pilot was a retired Air Force officer. Now there's a sign of real class: when your servants have servants!

Having accustomed myself to the squirrely controls, we made several flights around the central Texas area for a few days, but the guys were not happy with the results. The wind was too calm. We hopped up to Love Field and visited the Weather Bureau office there. It turned out there was a big stationary high-pressure area over the Midwest, with very light winds. The only place they could find with some wind was Wichita, Kansas.

The next morning, we packed up and headed to Wichita. Kuni went up with Ed, and I flew the Cherokee up alone. We based at a small airport east of town. Ironically, in this town made famous by Cessna and Beech, it was called Piper Airpark. It was owned and operated by a Piper dealer. It was very convenient, though, to some wide-open terrain to the northeast of town.

One day, while flying around some distance from the airport, Ed informed me that the probe needed some adjusting, and wondered if there was an airport close by where he could make a quick adjustment. I noticed on the chart that we were near a small field at El Dorado, Kan. I called them on Unicom (the common advisory frequency) to get an advisory. "No reported traffic," was the reply, "winds light and variable."

When I got there, though, I found the windsock standing straight out, and almost at a right angle to the runway. I banked way over and used nearly all the available rudder to keep it on the runway for a near-maximum-performance crosswind landing. While Ed worked on the probe, I went into the office and informed the young man operating the Unicom that the wind was anything but light and variable. "Yeah," he said, "that anemometer hasn't been working too well lately," pointing to the dial on the wall that indicated two or three knots.

A few minutes later, a Cessna pilot called in for a landing advisory, and the reply was, "No reported traffic. Winds light and variable." So much for reality.

After a few days in Kansas, Kuni was happy with the data obtained, and we headed for home. Kuni rode home with Ed, and I made the flight back solo. It was a Friday afternoon when I set out, hoping to reach St. Louis. A front was moving through that area, but was expected to clear out later in the afternoon. As I progressed, I kept checking the weather over the radio. The front was moving very slowly, and I began to search for an alternate airport. I was all set to turn south toward Jefferson City, but on one last-ditch effort, I called and found that St. Louis had just cleared, so I headed on in.

I landed at St. Louis-Lambert International, and taxied to the nearest FBO (there were several on the airport). The ramp was filled mostly with Learjets and Citations, but I was treated just as courteously as if I had been flying a multi-million-dollar jet. They found me a room in a Sheraton adjacent to the field, and ran me over in their van.

Trusting the forecast I had gotten the night before, I optimistically checked out the next morning, but I did stop at the flight service station. This was good, because it had not cleared as forecast. The front was still in the same place, and churning up lots of storms. The briefer showed me this on the live radar they had. I called to check back into the Sheraton, but there was no room. Same story at other motels. The only place I could get a room was at the Hilton. I took it, but wondered how it would look on my expense account when I checked out of a three-star motel to stay at the most expensive four-star place on the airport.

The weather was still the same the next day, but the third morning, I went over to flight service; the briefer at first gave me the same bad news, but then looked again, and said, "Wait a minute, aren't you trying to get in Victor 12 (airway)? There is a hole in the storms along that route right now. If you get out in the next hour, you should be okay."

I quickly filed a flight plan, checked out, and headed for the airplane. In less than an hour, I was climbing out through the low clouds and into an area between layers. I could see a storm to the north, with lightning flashing, and another to the south, but right where I was it was okay. How about that? It was just like it looked on the radar. That stuff really works.

I had filed to Indianapolis, where I took a look at the weather to the east. It looked a lot better, so I headed out from there VFR. This was a mistake, because as I approached the Dayton area, the clouds were building again, just as on a previous trip. Once again, I had to duel Mother Nature to out-climb her building clouds. I gave the Cherokee all the climb performance she had in her, and as before, I just barely won out, skimming the tops of the clouds until they finally descended into a lower layer to the east. I was beginning to think there was some angry weather god out to get me in this location. I made a note to check the area very carefully the next time I flew through here.

I landed at Columbus, and again filed IFR for the rest of the trip home. That was wise, and I made it no sweat, with an easy VOR approach into University Park.

Ed Jordan and Kuni repairing equipment during turbulence tests in Wichita, Kan.

Chapter Nine
Turbulence II

The next summer, the turbulence group had adjusted the theoretical model with the help of the previous flight tests, and were now ready to recheck it. Kuni had graduated, so the project was now under the direction of a new scientist in the Applied Research Lab on campus. He was a former Marine officer, and more serious and business-like than I was used to with Kuni. He picked the test location this time. It was Grand Forks, North Dakota. There was a weather tower just north of there on the Canadian border that was shared by the Canadian and American weather services. There was a balloon attached to it, which could measure ambient conditions even higher.

It was September before we got underway. I took the Cherokee up alone, and the day I was to depart, bad weather was hanging over the Great Lakes. I tried to skirt it to the south, but only got to Dayton. (I watched *Play Misty for Me* in the motel that night.)

The next day, the weather had greatly improved, so I made the first leg to Rockford, Ill. The FBO was very friendly, and even ran me across the field to the Holiday Inn for lunch in their restaurant. When I settled up the fuel bill, the manager gave me his business card. It read, "Rockford Aviation, James Johnson, Pres. Mon.-Wed.-Fri., Vice Pres. Tue.-Thur.-Sat." Interesting.

From there, it was a long, tedious trip up through Wisconsin along the Mississippi to Minneapolis. I landed at Minneapolis-St. Paul International expecting to find lots of motels for overnight lodging. There were, but they were all full. The FBO finally found me a hotel in downtown Minneapolis, and it was a long taxi ride in. As we approached town, the scene looked familiar, as I remembered Mary Tyler Moore throwing her hat up in the air to the music playing, "You're gonna make it after all." I didn't feel much like throwing my hat in the air. To me, I was headed for a desolate region of the country.

I called the crew, already in Grand Forks, and they told me that the Aviation Department at The University of North Dakota had given us some space in their large hangar. I made it up to Grand Forks in about two and a half hours, and had the tower direct me to the UND hangar. The guys were there, and immediately started to work on the airplane while I huddled in the corner of the cold hangar. There was no office here. My only consolation was that at least we didn't have to work out on the ramp.

The next day, we headed up toward the weather tower near Pembina VOR, but found that the balloon was not attached. Some vandals had cut it loose to drift away. The terrain was favorable for testing, though, and we proceeded to carry on.

Then it rained for two days, which was fine by me, because I had come down with a cold. We huddled in the rooms, and I got to see *Funny Girl* and *Tora Tora Tora* on HBO. Finally, it cleared up and my cold was better, so we resumed testing.

The Ramada Inn across the street had a marquis that read "Lawrence Welk Live Thursday Evening," I asked the desk clerk why Lawrence Welk would perform at this out-of-the-way place. He replied, "Oh, he's from North Dakota, and performs around the state whenever he has a chance. He's very loyal."

On Friday morning, as we loaded up to head to the airport, I noticed the sign was being changed. The Lawrence Welk notice was gone, and they were putting up letters that spelled, "Welcome Second Coming of Christ."

"Boy, they sure do get some celebrities in this little town!" one of the guys remarked. (Second Coming of Christ was actually the name of an organization convening there that weekend.)

By the end of that day, we had compiled enough data, and we packed up for home the next morning. I had an old girlfriend who was then going to law school in St. Paul, so I gave her a call to see if we might have dinner that evening. She agreed, so I decided to stop there for the night, even though it was a short hop on this long journey home. I asked her if she lived right in St. Paul, and when she said she did, I asked her if she knew where St. Paul Downtown Airport was. It looked very convenient on the chart. "I never heard of it," she replied.

"Okay, I'll go into Minneapolis-St. Paul."

"Oh, I know where that is," she proudly responded.

We had a nice dinner, and then went back to her apartment in a high-rise in the middle of St. Paul. While she was fixing some drinks or something, I wandered over to the window, and noticed a rotating green and white beacon about two blocks away. I looked down and saw blue taxiway lights. "Hey, Maria, come here," I said. "There's St. Paul Downtown Airport."

"Oh, yeah, I've seen airplanes flying around there," was her casual response.

The next day, bad weather had set in, as forecast. I had to pay for my overnight stop. I filed IFR to Madison, Wis. Plodding down along this route on Sunday morning, I was working Chicago Control Center, and I became aware that I hadn't heard a single call for some time. I thought perhaps I had lost contact, so I was about to call them, when I heard a voice on the frequency inquisitively say, "Hello?"

Then another voice responded with, "Hello."

I guess we all had the same concern, but now we were all sure we were still on, so there was no more radio activity until I got close to Madison. The ILS was out there, and I had to make a radar surveillance approach. This was the only time I can remember making an actual radar-guided approach, but it worked out okay.

The weather was worse to the east, but it looked like I could make it as far as Rockford, so I filed to there. It was a short hop, but it got me a little farther, and I remembered the convenient Holiday Inn there. At Rockford, I had to hold and make a back-course localizer approach. I had done these before, but it wasn't my favorite type of approach. It was a day for unusual approaches.

After a night at the Rockford Holiday Inn, I checked out and headed to the flight service station there. The briefer gave me a dire forecast of storms all along my route to the east. Resigned to another night in Rockford, I headed for a phone down the hall and called my office to inform them of the situation. On the way back, I decided to make a last stop at flight service to check on forecasts for the next few days. When I did, a new briefer had come on duty and asked if he could help me. I told him of my intended flight, but that it didn't look doable. He looked at the charts, and said, "Oh, I don't know about that. There are no storms reported right now, and what are expected to develop will be widely scattered. There isn't really much convective activity."

I decided that, between the two briefings, I'd take this one. I filed IFR, headed out to the airplane, did a quick preflight in light rain, and got under way. A few minutes later, I was cruising at 7000 feet between layers, and in very smooth air. I landed at Fort Wayne, where I again had to do a back-course localizer. This was really a challenging trip approach-wise.

It was IFR all the way home, and I had to do a VOR approach (the only one) into my home airport. I was glad that this trip was over. I had had enough of North Dakota, and of turbulence testing in general. Fortunately, it was my last experience with it.

Chapter Ten
A Copilot

By the early 1970's, I had come to like the academic life, and wanted to make a career of it. To really succeed in this field, however, you have to hold a doctoral degree, the "union card" of professors, as we refer to it. I had looked at several schools for a suitable program, and finally got one set up at The University of Virginia. In 1974, I secured a leave of absence from Penn State, and moved to Charlottesville for a year to complete my coursework. After that, I returned to Penn State and resumed teaching, while also working on a thesis.

I had to make frequent trips down to UVa, however, to consult with my advisor, make progress reports, and give some required presentations. By this time, the Department at Penn State had acquired a new Piper Arrow, and it came in very handy to make most of these trips. The five-hour drive was reduced to an hour and twenty minutes by air.

Around this time, I was also seriously dating a woman who worked in administration at Penn State, and I took her along on several of these trips. She seemed to like this mode of travel. In the summer of 1978, I received my final degree, and we got married a few months later.

My wife loved to fly with me, but had little desire to become a pilot herself. She did take a few formal lessons, though, and although she never soloed, she picked up the skills very quickly. She got good enough at holding heading and altitude that she could relieve me for other flight duties on long trips. I now had a copilot!

More importantly, I had a very nice traveling companion, so I began to plan some flights. I couldn't just take the department airplane anywhere at any time, but I could use it on business trips and make a stop or two along the way, even with small side trips. When such trips were to interesting places, I took my wife along.

The first such trip that I remember was to visit a transportation research institute in Cambridge, Mass. We flew up to Boston Logan one Thursday afternoon in June. Logan was the one large major airport that I visited where I was treated in a less than welcome manner. Most controllers at large airports were very friendly to small airplanes (I remember Dulles Approach Control inquiring what FBO I was headed to, and then working hard to put me on a runway that was convenient to it).

Maybe it was just the particular controllers on that particular day at Logan, but they seemed to be sort of annoyed with this small airplane. The ground controller seemed especially bothered by what I imagine he considered a green, low-time pilot who had no business at this big airport. I was merely trying to navigate my way across a complex network of taxiways at a totally unfamiliar airport. I was never bothered by such treatment, though, and always responded calmly and politely.

After my meeting on Friday morning, we headed out, as planned, to fly to Hyannis, and spend the weekend on Cape Cod. The first part of the plan, though, to make a scenic flight down the coast, had to be scrubbed. A low cloud layer had moved in over the Cape, and I had to file IFR to get down through it.

Otis AFB Approach Control handled instrument traffic at Hyannis and told me to expect the ILS approach. Just as I got it all set up, they came back and told me that due to traffic, they would have to give me the NDB (non-directional beacon) approach. As I was frantically cranking around on the ADF, they again changed the plan, and cleared me to the ILS. As they were giving me the clearance, I noticed the localizer needle starting to center, so I had to quickly start the approach.

I should have aborted and tried it when I was better prepared, but I continued inbound and soon broke out, but about a half mile off the centerline. I was able to make a quick S-turn, and get on the runway, though, for a decent landing. As we taxied in, my wife said, "How come we were so far off the runway when we broke out?"

"Well, sometimes the ILS is not that accurate," I responded, while thinking to myself, *And sometimes the pilot isn't!* She had great confidence in my flying ability, so I didn't want to do anything to diminish it.

We had a nice weekend touring the Cape, taking a harbor cruise and dining on lobster and clam chowder (the best I have ever tasted). Before we left the area, we hopped over to Martha's Vineyard, looked around Edgartown, and had lunch at a nice restaurant overlooking the harbor. Then, I called Flight Service for a briefing on VFR to our home base.

Boston FSS gave me a warning of numerous thunderstorms all through Pennsylvania. To get a better picture, I made a long distance call to my home FSS (flight service station), Phillipsburg. When I heard a familiar voice there, I said, "Hey, Tom, I'm up here on Martha's Vineyard, and getting dire warnings from Boston about thunderstorms down that way. What's happening?"

"Oh, yeah," he replied, "there are the usual storm warnings that we get around here in the summertime, but I don't expect much to develop. If they do, they'll be widely scattered."

Those were the good old days when a briefer could give you his opinion, based on years of experience with the local weather, rather than just read the published forecasts. I took this briefing rather than Boston's. We flew home and didn't see a single storm.

A few years later, I had to attend a conference in Atlanta that looked like it could double as a mini-vacation, so my wife got a little time off and went along. It was during the controllers strike, and unfortunately, the weather was turning bad the day we were to leave. A strong cold front was moving in from the west all along our route. During the strike, you had to get a reservation for an IFR flight. Only a certain number were approved in a given area each hour.

I couldn't get a reservation until late in the day—too late to avoid the storms, or even to set out on a trip of this length. I decided to risk VFR, and deviate as far east as was practical to at least get part way that day. By the time I got south of Washington, however, the clouds were really building, and an attempt to climb over them appeared fruitless. I spiraled down through a hole to get under them, and decided to head for Charlottesville.

I had to get right down on the deck, though, to stay VFR, so I handed my wife the chart, pointed to our approximate position, and told her to check for high towers or other obstruction between there and C-ville. For a non-pilot, she could read charts pretty well. We made it okay (although maybe not with legal minimum altitude), and over-nighted in Charlottesville. By the time we got through dinner, the storms hit, and I was very glad to be on the ground.

The next day, it cleared up rapidly, and we were far enough south to make it to Atlanta in one hop. We landed at Dekalb-Peachtree Airport on the north side of town, a very busy, but friendly, general aviation hub. We got to the conference in time for lunch, and only missed the activities of the first morning.

After a few days with some enjoyable side trips, the conference ended, and we prepared to depart for home. The weather was VFR all the way to Pennsylvania, but the wind was churning up something fierce. I had to climb up to 9,500 feet to get out of bad turbulence, but up there the wind was very strong out of the northwest, almost a direct crosswind. I ended up holding such a large wind correction angle, that I didn't have much thrust left along our course. My normal 130-knot cruise in the Arrow was reduced to under 100. It was slow progress.

I had to find a fuel stop that was within my range, and, also have a runway pretty much into the wind. Winston-Salem filled the bill. The landing was a little challenging, but doable. Once on the ground, I seriously considered just aborting the rest of the trip until the next day, but a chance event changed my mind. Two guys in a Piper Seneca landed right after me, and when they came into the office, I asked them where they had come from. "Bloomsburg, Pa," was the reply.

That's not far from my destination, so I pressed them for details on the weather up that way. "Oh, you'll have a good tailwind," the one guy said, "because we had a helluva headwind coming down."

That seemed strange, but I thought maybe the winds had shifted around since the forecast I had gotten, so we set out again. This time, our forward progress was even slower, and I deduced what prompted the Seneca pilot's prediction. He didn't have a headwind, but was encountering the same strong crosswind that we were, so it seemed like a headwind because of the large yaw angle required.

I had to go to 11,500 feet to get out of turbulence, and again started to look for a spot to land and stop overnight. I checked the ATIS (automatic terminal information system) at Dulles, but they were reporting winds of forty knots, gusting to fifty. Forget that! I continued on to Harrisburg, where I was familiar, and knew there was a runway 30 that would put us pretty much into the wind. That worked, even though the surface wind was thirty-two knots. We stayed with friends in Harrisburg that night, and made the easy last hop the next morning. Another memorable trip!

Chapter Eleven
To the Islands

Ever since I started flying, I longed to fly to the Bahamas. Stories of such flights often appeared in the aviation magazines, and I was always intrigued by them. Those illustrated with a Bonanza or Cessna sitting under a glistening palm in front of a white sandy beach were even more enticing. The Bahamas were an ideal pilot's destination. They were close enough to Florida to be reached by almost any light airplane, yet far enough away to make a flight there somewhat of a challenging adventure.

In the summer of 1980, I was registered to attend a conference at the Florida Institute of Technology in Melbourne, Fla. This was as close as I would come to the Bahamas on a scheduled trip. I conceived a plan to fly down to the conference, and then take a few more days and hop over to the Islands. I figured I could get away with this "slight deviation" on my business trip in the company airplane. I ran the idea by my wife to accompany me on this jaunt, and she was up for it. She managed to get two weeks off during this period, and I booked the Department's Piper Arrow. We were all set for what was to be our greatest flying adventure yet.

I studied the travel brochures and the pilots' guides to Bahamas flying. I determined that the most convenient route to the Bahamas was the so-called "northern route," which takes you to Grand Bahama Island. The western end is only 55 nm from the Florida shoreline, and another 17 miles takes you to Freeport, the major town on the island. Freeport, like Nassau, has a VOR, which simplifies navigation considerably. But, also like Nassau, it is a major tourist attraction with airline service. Thousands of tourists converge there each year to gamble in the casinos and shop at the International Bazaar. This was not the unspoiled, primitive haven from civilization that I was looking for. For such atmosphere, I had to go to one of the so-called "out islands."

The Abacos qualify in this category, and are just east of Grand Bahama. Great Abaco, the largest of this group, has two major settlements with airports. One of these is Marsh Harbor, with a 5000-foot runway. Marsh Harbor serves primarily as a haven for boaters, and has just a few locally-owned motels clustered around the harbor. I zeroed in on this destination and made a reservation at the Conch Inn, a ten-unit facility advertised as very natural, but nice. It was owned by an Englishman named Wally Smith, who could possibly be a distant relative from my Anglo-Saxon heritage. (Maybe that influenced my choice.)

The conference began on a Monday, so we set out the previous Friday for a leisurely tour down the coast. We flew to Myrtle Beach, about as far south along the coast as I could go non-stop. We landed at Grand Strand Airport, which is actually in North Myrtle Beach, and got a room in a beachside motel.

The next day, I had planned to make a scenic flight down along the coast to Daytona Beach, where we would stop for the next night. When I checked the weather that morning, however, I found that a low, solid cloud layer covered the shore from just south of us down into northern Florida. Daytona was clear, though, so I could go VFR, but the aerial tour of Charleston, Savannah, and Brunswick turned out to be a monotonous trek over an endless blanket of billowy white (just like our trip to Cape Cod).

The clouds broke around Jacksonville, as forecast, so we did get to see some shoreline down past St. Augustine and Flagler, and into Daytona. I had made reservations at The Inn at Indigo Lakes, a plush resort inn at the time, built around a small scenic lake with tennis courts, jogging trails, and a large pool in a tropical garden setting. We landed at Daytona International and got a ride over to the Inn in their van. Indigo was not far from the airport. We spent a relaxing rest of the day lounging around the pool and dining at the very nice restaurant next door.

Early the next day, we headed back to the airport to hop down to Melbourne before the ubiquitous Florida summer thunderstorms developed. Unfortunately, it wasn't early enough. As we climbed out, I could see thick cumulus clouds rapidly building up ahead. I deviated inland in an effort to get around them, but to no avail. I then tried to top them, but also gave up on this try at around 12,000 feet. I had no alternative but to try to get under them. I looked for some breaks in the clouds and tried to weave my way down through.

Eventually, I did get underneath, but I had lost track of my position with all the zigzagging, and I found myself right over a very large airport. It was Orlando International! I certainly didn't belong there, so I scooted out to the southeast as fast as I could, without a word to anyone on the radio. I found that I could stay under the clouds at around 1000 feet above the ground.

Even though we were still pretty far out, I called Melbourne Approach. They came back loud and clear, gave me a transponder code, and then informed me they had me on radar. They gave me a heading to Melbourne, and even advised me that they saw no storms between me and the airport. That was a relief, and the rest of the flight was just as relaxing as the beginning was anxious.

At Melbourne, we parked at the FBO and got a taxi over to FIT. The campus was very nice, with lots of palm trees and other tropical foliage. There was even a large tropical botanical garden, which served as both an academic facility and a tourist attraction. We took advantage of this latter role that afternoon. It was a very fascinating walk on the scenic paths through the jungle. The only warning to tourists was to watch for reptiles. We didn't encounter any.

The conference was very nice and family friendly, with a cookout in a beachside pavilion one evening, and a guided tour of the Kennedy Space Center one afternoon. We also got away one day, rented a car, and drove over to Disney World. There was only the Magic Kingdom at that time, but it was exciting even for adults who were first-time visitors like us.

The conference wound down a bit ahead of time on Thursday, so early Friday morning we set out for St. Lucie County Airport at Ft. Pierce for the next, and most memorable, phase of our trip. Ft. Pierce was the northernmost gateway airport to the Bahamas. There was a customs office there, and next to that was Ft. Pierce Flying Service, which provided all kinds of service to pilots going to the Islands. There were lots of forms to be completed for this international flight, and they had a supply of them. They also rented survival equipment, some of which was required.

I had expected to spend much of the day filling out forms and making other preparations, so I intended to leave the next day. Ft. Pierce informed us, however, that they would assist us with the forms, and could have us on our way in half an hour. Since it was still morning, I decided to accept that suggestion. One small problem arose in that I had no room reservation that night, but the FBO called around and found us a room in Lucaya, an adjunct of Freeport. That would provide a break in the trip, so it seemed welcome.

I then went over to the survival equipment desk and asked for two life vests and a raft. They had plenty of vests, but were all out of rafts. "The vests are all that are required, and all you really need," the girl at the counter said. "That route is highly traveled by both planes and boats. If anything were to happen, you'd be picked up right away. You'd hardly be in the water at all."

With that reassurance, I took the vests, filed my flight plan (required), and we headed out for our hop over the pond. There was an airway that went out from Vero Beach VOR, and gradually diverged from shore to an intersection called Bluffi. This seemed like an excellent way to become accustomed to over-water flight while still in sight of shore. At Bluffi, I could tune in the Freeport VOR, and go there direct on the radial that I would be on.

I climbed up to 9,500 feet to get as much glide distance as I could. I figured that I would only be out of range of either Florida or Grand Bahama for a few minutes in the middle of the route. At that altitude, we were well above the sea, and with the slight haze that prevailed over the water, we lost all sense of the fact that we were over the ocean. I don't remember experiencing any anxiety about being so far from land.

Things went pretty smoothly until I heard a distant call of "Pan, pan, pan!" on the FSS frequency. Pan is the international call for help when the emergency doesn't quite warrant a full-fledged Mayday. I reached for the mike to respond, but some flight service responded before I could. "I am lost over the ocean, and running low on fuel," I heard the pilot tell flight service just before he faded out completely. I believe that I would have called a full Mayday in that situation.

In a few minutes more, I saw some land ahead, and then I could make out an airport. It was the private field at West End Settlement on Grand Bahama. "There it is," I said excitedly to my wife, "There's West End!"

She calmly looked down at the chart and put her finger on West End. In flying many hours with me, she had acquired the ability to read charts pretty well. As we reached the shore, I gave Freeport Tower a call and advised them of my intentions to land.

Freeport seemed extremely concerned about traffic separation and asked for my position several times. My replies were relayed to a Cessna, and his position was repeatedly given to me. I eventually learned that the Cessna 172 was about five miles ahead of me and the only other traffic. He was taxiing in when I first caught sight of the airport.

Needless to say, our landing was uneventful, without any threat of a mid-air. The runway at Freeport is 11,000 feet long and way out from the terminal. While negotiating the long drive on the taxiway, I inquired about closing my flight plan, and was advised, "Close flight plan on landing."

I wasn't sure if it had been closed by the tower, or that I was supposed to take some action to close it. I finally learned that, indeed, it was closed automatically, just like an IFR plan in the States. When we reached the ramp, I found it crowded with every imaginable type of light airplane, including jets. It seemed just like any major American airport. We had not yet escaped from civilization.

A line attendant meets every arriving airplane and ushers you direct to customs. Here, we were confronted by three very black, very bored-looking, but very official native customs agents. The first agent mumbled something, which I couldn't understand due to the blaring rock music coming from a radio in the corner of the small hot room. The response to my request to repeat that was equally unintelligible, so I just plunked down all of the paperwork that I had with me. I was told not to antagonize these agents because they take their jobs very seriously.

The agent sorted through the forms, handed back our birth certificates, and motioned to the next agent. He studied the forms very carefully, filled in some, and then handed them to the third agent. He stamped the forms, handed them back to me, and then put little stickers on all of our bags. Their duties seemed to be clearly segregated. I figured they had a union. Other than the first agent's mumble, none of them spoke a word or showed any sort of emotion.

Leaving the customs office, I stopped by the FBO (or whatever they call it), registered, and ordered fuel. We were then confronted by a host of taxi drivers, all eager for our business. I selected one, and we were whisked off to the Atlantic Beach Hotel in Lucaya. It was just after noon, so we spent the rest of the day lounging in the sun on the hotel's private beach.

The next day dawned bright and clear, as most do in this part of the world, so after breakfast, we headed to the airport for the last leg of our trip. I stopped by the customs office to inquire about the proper procedure to hop to another island, and was issued a "transire." This form is for inter-island travel once you have initially cleared customs.

After paying for the gas and parking, we started across the ramp, and I called the tower for taxi instructions. "Confirm that you have a flight plan on file," was the reply. I replied, "Negative," since the flying guide had indicated that none is required for travel between islands, except from Nassau. Apparently this info was outdated.

"Either file a flight plan by radio, or return to the office and call flight service," was the clear order.

Since he gave me the option of doing it by radio, I switched over to flight service, filed, and then immediately called ground control for another try, this time advising that I was on file to

Marsh Harbor. I was cleared to taxi right away, and the rest of the tower conversations went smoothly.

Marsh harbor is almost directly east of Freeport, so I tuned in the 90 degree radial of Freeport VOR, and proceeded eastbound. This course also parallels the south shore of Grand Bahama, so it was almost impossible to get lost. Good thing, because below there was nothing but trees—no towns, no roads or anything. I topped a 4000-foot scattered layer, and leveled at 5500 feet (the same cruising altitude rules apply as in the U.S.).

We passed the eastern end of Grand Bahama about forty miles from Nassau, and started over open water once again. The Freeport VOR signal was becoming a little unreliable, but I had a good heading established by now, so I just continued on it. In a short while, we approached the western shore of Abaco, and the features matched those on the chart remarkably, giving more validity to my navigation. If I thought Grand Bahama was wild, this island was worse. I didn't see any sign of civilization. I was beginning to wonder what I was doing out here!

The first thing I spotted other than forest was what appeared to be a runway in the distance. It had to be Marsh Harbor. As we got closer, I was sure that it was an airport, and its east-west orientation pretty much verified it as Marsh Harbor. There was no other sign of life, however, just this 5000-foot strip of concrete. I called unicom, but there was no answer. Both the chart and the flying guide indicated that one was available. Then an Aztec also called for Marsh Harbor Unicom, again with no answer. Then, out of nowhere, an unknown voice said, "Marsh Harbor has no Unicom."

Another bit of outdated information. I checked the wind sock and set up for a landing to the west. As we taxied in, I saw my first signs of any life here: a small line shack and a few airplanes parked around it. They were hidden from the air by dense trees. I taxied up in front of it and shut down.

We were met by an exuberant young native, who apparently was the line boy. He was all set to usher us to customs, when he spotted the stickers on our luggage. "Oh, you go right on through," he announced jubilantly. He seemed to be happier about this than we were, apparently because it relieved him of some of his duties.

I expressed my desire to see that the airplane was secure first. I had brought a tie-down kit for just such a location. "Just leave it there," he said. "I take care of it."

He said this with such conviction that I took his word for it, and went on inside. The customs agents here seemed almost pleasant, and nodded politely when they saw the stickered luggage. They seemed as anxious to avoid any duties as the line boy was. There was even a taxi waiting at this somewhat desolate terminal, and in few minutes, we were being ushered into our room at the Conch Inn.

The room was not plush, but clean and quaint, with a patio overlooking the harbor—just what you would want in this location. As we checked in, we met a young couple who were just checking out of our room. They had just returned from their first sailing trip and were anxious for receptive ears to hear of their adventures. We went over to the coffee shop for lunch with them, where we met another couple who had just arrived in their own yacht. They were retired, sailing around over the world and tying up wherever they took a notion to. We found this way of life to be typical of the other boat couples that we met here. We listened to their stories with great fascination.

Then they turned to us and ask how we had gotten there. When I told them we had flown in on an airplane that we had piloted, they expressed equal interest in us, and wanted to know all about our trip. I was somewhat surprised, but pleased, to be the center of attention among this fascinating group of adventurers.

The next few days were just delightful, as we indulged in the atmosphere of total relaxation that prevailed here. We rented bicycles that were available from the inn, and rode around exploring the tiny village and its surroundings. The only warning we were given was to watch out for wild boars (we didn't see any).

Wally Smith, the owner, takes great pains to see that your stay is pleasant. He seems to be everywhere, checking chlorine in the pool, serving ice cream cones, taking radio calls from boats, etc. In the afternoon, he puts a net across the middle of the pool, and the boat people assemble to play a water-immersed version of volleyball. They call it "Wallyball." There was really no beach, but we really didn't miss it, since the pool was in a delightful setting, surrounded by tropical foliage, with hyacinth and bougainvillea flowers in bloom.

In the evenings, we would stroll over to the Conch Inn dining room, remotely located next to the Conch Out Bar (Conch is pronounced "Conk"). The dining room overlooks the harbor, and has an island atmosphere, complete with wicker chairs and ceiling fans ala Casablanca. I almost expected to hear Sam playing the piano. The seafood here was among the best I have ever eaten, the superb cracked conch and broiled crawfish (the tropical version of lobster) were almost worth the trip alone.

After dinner, we would take a leisurely stroll along the harbor and back to the room. The day was topped off with a generous serving of Bahamian sunset, sparkling the waters of the harbor and backlighting the boats bobbing on their moors.

As all good things must, our visit came to an end. On the day of our departure, we checked out early, and went over to the coffee shop for breakfast. I saw some clouds building up in a direction that I determined to be west, our intended course. By the second cup of coffee, they had built up into genuine thunderstorms. I called Flight Service, but info out here was sketchy, and there was no mention of storms. I decided to give it a try, and got a taxi out to the field. It began to rain on the way.

At the airport, I could clearly see two storms to the west, one just north of the field, and the other more to the south. I watched a Bonanza take off, and head west—he didn't come back. Then a Navajo landed, and taxied in. I watched for the pilot to exit, and asked him about the weather. He said indeed there were storms right there, but they were avoidable, and just a few miles to the west, it was clear all the way to Florida. Then a Comanche took off and headed for a pass between the storms. I decided to head out and see for myself. If we couldn't get through, we could turn around and come back.

We walked out to the airplane, and I found the line boy's "secure tie-down" consisted of pushing the airplane back into the grass, and placing a rock in front of the nosewheel. Too late to worry about that now. Fortunately, there had been no storms while we were there. I preflighted pretty thoroughly, then we loaded up and headed out.

I made a circle of the field, both to gain altitude, and to better view the storms. The valley between the storms was still there, so I headed toward it, climbing as much as I could. At about 7500 feet, we reached the clouds, and I thought at first I would top them, but then we plunged into them. "Don't worry," I said to my wife, "we'll be through this in a few seconds." (Or so I hoped.)

The seconds dragged on to several very long minutes, and I began to wonder about the wisdom of this action. I was reminded of the similar bout with the storms below Dayton many years ago, but then I wasn't 200 miles out in the Atlantic. Then, suddenly we broke out, and just as the Navajo pilot had said, it looked clear as far as I could see ahead. I called Nassau Radio and opened my flight plan to Ft. Pierce.

I climbed up to 10,500 feet and picked up the Freeport VOR. Passing Freeport, I stayed on that radial and headed directly for West Palm Beach, the shortest route to the mainland. The trip back seemed much quicker than the one out, and in about a half hour from Grand Bahama, I could see the Florida coastline. I continued directly to it, and then turned up the coast toward Ft. Pierce.

I called Vero Beach Radio and gave them an update on my ETA. Customs uses this info to keep track of you, and they like to know exactly when to expect you. As we taxied in at the reported time, an agent was waiting for us on the customs ramp. The U.S. agents are a bit friendlier than their Bahamian cousins, but every bit as serious. Drug smuggling has become a big issue.

When they asked us if we had anything to declare, all I could think of was a bottle of Coca Cola, so I think they realized that we were honest tourists. They released us pretty quickly, and we taxied over to the FBO to turn in our life vests, and get lunch in the snack bar there.

We then headed up the coast toward Pennsylvania, with an overnight stop at Charleston. As we cruised along at 9500 feet on top of the scattered layer, I felt relaxed and content that I had successfully negotiated this great flight that went pretty much as planned. I felt a little let down, though, knowing that it was all over, and that the only remaining task was a routine flight home.

West End on Grand Bahama, our first sight of land in the islands.

My wife (at the time) Esther and I relaxing at the Conch Inn in Marsh harbor.

Chapter Twelve
Juliet

In 1983, I was invited to spend a year as a Visiting Professor at Embry-Riddle Aeronautical University in Daytona Beach. I had visited there before, and was always fascinated by this school that was totally absorbed in aviation. Hey, it was even located on an airport! I secured a sabbatical leave, and my wife got a leave of absence for most of the year. We flew down in the Arrow to meet with the faculty there, and find a place to live. She was impressed with the red-carpet treatment at Florence, S.C. The FBO there at the time would meet each airplane and spread a small red carpet out under the wing for you to step down onto.

In August, we moved into a nice, fairly new apartment on a small lake near the campus. My wife then had to return to Penn State for a few months at the beginning of the school year, but was able to join me in November. In the meantime, I spent my free time taking sailing lessons and hanging out at New Smyrna Beach Airport, a few miles south of Daytona.

New Smyrna was an uncontrolled field, and, although fairly busy, it was very friendly and sort of laid back. A lot of local pilots hung out in the FBO there, and I was readily accepted as one of them. I checked out in the Tomahawk that the FBO had and flew around the area a bit, but it was often booked for flight training.

I started to look for a small, cheap airplane to buy. I decided that it would be something to fly while down there, and then I would sell it when I left. I tried out an old Piper Colt and a Grumman Trainer. When my wife arrived, however, she seemed disappointed that I was looking for a two-place. "Why don't you look for a four-place?" she asked. "That way, we could take friends and family along."

I told her that it would cost more, but she seemed to think that it would be worth it. How many wives urge you to buy a more expensive airplane? Her interest in my buying an airplane, however, may have been influenced by her sailing experience. When she first arrived, I was anxious to show off my new sailing "skills," so we went sailing on the Halifax River a few weekends. When I suggested going again on a later Saturday, she was apparently fed up with my less-than-perfect sailing expertise, and said, "Why don't we go flying? You know how to do that."

I started to look for a good four-place at a reasonable price (I couldn't afford a new Bonanza). I located a Cherokee 180C that had just been pretty much rebuilt by the A&P owner, with a newly majored engine and a professional Imron paint job in the latest Piper style. It was only 100 miles away in Brooksville, FL, over on the west coast.

We flew over in a rented 172 one weekend. While wandering around the airport, my wife pointed to an airplane in an open T-hangar, and said, "There's a really nice looking one."

I looked, and saw that it was a Cherokee. "I believe that's it," I responded.

As we got closer, I saw the tail number, 9663J. "It is!" I added.

The owner came a few minutes later, and gave us a demo ride. We both fell in love with it, and I gave the guy a deposit. After I scraped together the rest of the money, one of my students flew me over in his Cessna 150 (he gave flight instruction in it), and I picked up "Juliet," as I came to call her.

The first trip that I planned was to Key West. Like the Bahamas, I had also yearned to fly there. So, one long weekend when I could get off on Friday, we departed early and flew down the coast. At Miami, I climbed up to 8,500 feet to get over the

TCA (Terminal Control Area, now called Class B airspace). To be courteous, and also as a precaution, I called Miami Approach Control and reported my position. They came back and gave me a discrete transponder code, and added, "We're going to vector you to align you with the traffic."

What traffic? I didn't see another airplane anywhere. They turned me east, and headed me out over Biscayne Bay. I wanted to go southwest. Finally, after what seemed like an eternity, they turned me around and told me to resume my own navigation on course. All of this took about an extra fifteen minutes, but I like to be cooperative.

I dropped down to a lower altitude to take in the sights, and, for a first-timer, it was awesome to fly down the chain of keys and the long bridges that connect them. Key West is a long way down there, I found out. It was almost a three-hour trip starting from the middle of Florida. Fortunately, the weather was perfectly clear.

We landed at what is somewhat of a sprawling airport, and got a taxi into our motel on the south shore. Key West is just a delightful place for a couple of tourists like us, and small enough that you can walk almost anywhere you want to go. We took a guided tram tour of town and visited the Southernmost Point, the Lighthouse, the Maritime Museum, and, of course, the Hemingway House (my favorite). One afternoon, while sipping pina coladas, we listened to a Jimmy Buffet imitator in a beachside bar. Noticing his pale skin, I asked him if he had just arrived. "No, I was born here," he said, "but we locals stay out of the sun. It's just the tourists who get tanned."

Sadly, Sunday afternoon, we had to pack up and leave. I traced the island chain and the coast back up home over the same route that we came down. This time, though, when I crossed over the Miami TCA (at 9,500 feet), I didn't call anybody. And, once again, I didn't see any other airplane.

The next trip was very short but interesting. The local pilots had a custom of flying down to the Cape Canaveral area when there is a shuttle launch and watching it from the air. In those days, the restricted airspace was much less extensive, and you could circle around the Titusville area. I joined in this parade for the next launch. It was a spectacular sight from the air, and I even got a few pictures. Later, though, I thought about how dangerous this was for a dozen or more airplanes to be circling in a gaggle, all staring at what is happening a few miles to the east.

I had planned a few more flights around Florida and a possible return to the Bahamas, but time ran out on us. At the end of May, reluctantly, we had to return to our northern home. After getting settled, I located a hangar at the old Air Depot, a grass field on the edge of State College. I got an airline ticket to Daytona and went down one weekend to retrieve Juliet. She was too good an airplane to regard just as an interim one during my southern stay. I made it back in two legs, with a stop in Fayetteville, N.C.

I soon recognized my wife's wisdom in opting for a four-place. The couple we were best friends with also liked to fly, so the four of us made a number of enjoyable trips. No longer did I have to tie the trips in with business. On our first jaunt, we flew down to Tangier Island in the Chesapeake. This quaint little settlement is a transplanted New England fishing village, reachable only by boat or small airplane.

After walking around the town and having a crab cake fest for lunch (all you could eat, family style), we proceeded down the bay and across to southern Virginia and North Carolina. We landed next at First Flight Airport at Kittyhawk. This unattended strip is right at the base of the Wright Brothers Memorial, and very close to the field where the first successful flights were made. After touring that historic and sacred (to aviators) spot, we then flew up to Patrick Henry Airport and spent the night at a motel in Hampton. (I had more of the delicious Maryland crab cakes for dinner.) The next day, we drove up to Williamsburg and wandered around the historic district and Merchants' Square. In late afternoon, we flew back home in time for dinner. It's amazing what you can do in two days in a light airplane!

The next summer, the four of us flew up to Martha's Vineyard for a long weekend. The Vineyard is normally a single-leg trip of about three hours. We stayed in a new motel just outside Edgartown and drove all around the island. One day, we hopped over to Nantucket and spent the day touring that delightful town.

Then the weather turned bad, and I had to file IFR for the return trip. The remnants of a front were still hanging through New York, and the headwinds were fierce. I even had to make a fuel stop in Williamsport. Since I was still based at an airport with no approach, I always filed to University Park. I would shoot the ILS, and if I broke out high enough, I would cancel IFR and fly on over to the Air Depot VFR.

This trick worked at another destination. We frequently flew up to visit my wife's folks in Warren, Pa. I usually landed at a small grass strip called Brokenstraw (after the creek it was located on). If the weather was bad, I would file IFR to Jamestown, N.Y., and shoot the approach there, then cancel and proceed to Brokenstraw. My plan B, in the event the weather was too low, was to go ahead and land, and then call my father-in-law to pick us up. Jamestown was not that far away. Fortunately, I never had to resort to this alternative.

Getting the red carpet treatment in Florence, N. C.

Esther and I with Juliet, shortly after we purchased her in Florida.

Chapter Thirteen

The Later Years

My flying was considerably curtailed in the late '80's, when I developed some heart problems and ended up having bypass surgery. I have a glider rating, so I reverted to that mode of aviating, since it didn't require a medical certificate. In the meantime, I pursued a special issuance medical, which, after much effort, I acquired in 1988.

Unfortunately, I lost it again a few years later when I failed to show good results in the tests that the FAA required. I had to go through these every year. I became aware that motor gliders were officially gliders, as far as the FAA was concerned, and also did not require a medical certificate. Some of them are also half decent airplanes in the cruising mode. I began my search for one.

I located a Grob G109 in very good condition in Phoenix, Ariz. Early one Saturday morning, I set out, via airlines, to Phoenix. I arrived well before noon, Phoenix time, and the owner picked me up. He gave me a very thorough demo ride and checkout. He was an old German fighter pilot and a retired General Motors automobile designer, who described himself as a "poor millionaire living in a community of rich millionaires." When he took me out to his house after the flying, I decided that I would be very happy to live in the style of a "poor millionaire."

He turned out to be a very generous man also. Sensing that I was nowhere near even the poor millionaire category, he offered me the aircraft at a bargain price. It was an offer that I couldn't refuse, so I gave him a down payment. When I got the rest of the money together and negotiated the transfer of ownership, I located an airline pilot who ferried airplanes in his spare time. He flew it to Pennsylvania in only two and a half days.

To help defray the cost, I sold a half share in the Cherokee, not wishing to relinquish it altogether. Then, I had to get an official checkout and endorsement in motor gliders from a glider examiner. Fortunately, the owner of the nearby glider port qualified.

The Grob was a fun airplane. It resembled a typical taildragger airplane, but with a great big wing. It cruised at about 90 knots, and could fly several hundred miles with its fuel-efficient 80hp Limbach engine. It had a full gyro panel and a nav/com that included glideslope. I even filed IFR a few times when the weather was marginal, but not solid IFR. I had to be careful what airports I went into, though, since its 55 ft span didn't fit well on all runways and taxiways.

Then, in 1994, my cardiologist gave me a new type of ultrasonic test and informed me that my heart looked pretty good in this. I gathered copies of the reports, sent them to the FAA, and within a year, had my special issuance medical back. The next year, when it looked as if I was going to retain the certificate, I sold the Grob and bought back the half share in Juliet. I was very glad that I had decided to hang onto her. I really yearned for a "real" airplane again.

About that same time, the Penn State administration decided that operation of aircraft by departments or other university entities was too risky, litigation-wise. So we were forced to sell the Arrow, despite the fact that we had operated airplanes for over thirty years without a single incident. Up to that time, I was still flying the Arrow on business, when I was medically certified.

The last long trip I made in that airplane was to Lakeland, FL. to give a talk at the Sun 'n Fun spring fly-in. I also made a stop in Savannah to visit Gulfstream on cooperative education business. It took longer to get through my meeting at Gulfstream than I expected, so I didn't get on my way to Lakeland until afternoon.

By that time, the weather had gone down between Jacksonville and Orlando, so I had to file IFR. I had a car reserved at Lakeland, but my late departure meant I would arrive after the air show had started, when the field would be closed. Hence, I filed to Winter Haven. I called there and found that the FBO had a few older rental cars, so I reserved one of those.

When I landed at Winter Haven, a Stinson Voyager landed right behind me and tied down next to me. There were two good ole boys from Georgia in it, and they were also going to Sun 'n Fun. They asked me where I was from, and when I told them Pennsylvania, one replied, "Pennsylvania? Whooee, you really did get a wild-ass whim to come all this way!"

I told them I had a reason to be there, and then I checked out my rental car (sort of a clunker). While loading up, I offered the Georgia boys a ride over to Lakeland. "No, Sir," they said, "we're going to fly over after the air show and camp under the wing."

The battery was a little weak in the Ford, but it started. As I pulled out of the airport, the ashtray, housing and all, fell out of the dashboard and landed on the floor. I didn't need it anyway. The car was no luxury model, but I didn't expect it to be at the price I paid.

I found that the motel I was staying at in Lakeland was closer to Winter Haven Airport than Lakeland Airport. Not a bad alternate. Since it was late afternoon, I didn't go out to the show that day; instead, I settled in and went in to take a relaxing shower. When I came out, it was pouring rain. It kept that up all evening, and into the night. I couldn't help but think about the Georgia boys. To this day, I wonder what they did.

My presentation went well the next day (Friday), and I got to take in a lot of the show. That night, I didn't sleep well at all, and had almost nightmare-like dreams. When I got up the next morning, I felt even worse. I started to go out to the air show, but turned around and went back to bed. I spent all day on my back watching HBO. I watched *Crocodile Dundee* for the first time. I only got up to drag over to the restaurant for a little soup. I kept thinking, *Well, it'll be interesting to see how I get out of this one.*

I turned in for the night at 7:00 in the evening and slept until 7:00 the next morning. I felt a world better—not completely well, but well enough so that I decided to try heading home. It was the day I had planned to depart. I had some toast for breakfast, coaxed the Ford to start one more time, and headed for Winter Haven. On the way, I picked up a loaf of whole wheat bread and a liter of Coke.

The weather was IFR again around Orlando, so I had to file a flight plan. I didn't need this complication yet. Flight Service told me to take off VFR, and pick up my clearance in the air from Tampa Approach Control. It was the day after the air show ended, and IFR flights were leaving from there, Lakeland, Tampa, and other places. I had to circle in the VFR pocket around that area waiting for a break in the conversations, but eventually I got to chime in, got my clearance, and was on my way.

I had only filed to Savannah, thinking that if I wasn't really up to going all the way, I could stop there overnight. It was a handy stop with two motels right on the field. I was only in IFR weather a short while, so I cancelled my flight plan half way to Savannah. I also was feeling better, so I proceeded on to Florence. I had some more of the bread I was munching on, with some jelly I had saved from breakfast, drank about a glass of Coke, and then headed home. I climbed up to 9,500 feet into smooth air, flipped on the autopilot, and sat back and rode along. For some reason, when not feeling 100 percent, I always feel a lot better in the air.

The Grob motorglider, an interesting experience.

Chapter Fourteen
Farewell Juliet, Hello Sierra

My last long flight in Juliet came a few years later. I retired from the University in 1999. Although I continued to teach a course every semester or two, I had a lot more free time. My wife and I had also split up by this time, giving me even more freedom. So, I decided to make a trip to Daytona to visit my old Embry-Riddle friends.

With a very flexible schedule, I waited for a large high-pressure area to move in from the west, so that I could ride the southerly tailwinds it produced on the east side. This plan worked even better than I had hoped. On the first leg to Florence, I was indicating almost 150 knots groundspeed on the GPS. I made it there in three hours flat.

On the second leg to Daytona, the wind died down a bit, but I still had some tailwind all the way. I made the whole trip in six hours flying time, a distance of almost 800 miles. Not bad for a Cherokee! I checked into my favorite Inn at Indigo (now a Holiday Inn), and had several days of relaxation on the shore.

Then the high, which was still holding up, was forecast to move off the coast the next day, and be followed by a number of days of bad weather. I decided to leave the next morning. I could even take advantage of the northerly push on the west side of the high. I awoke to the alarm at 0600 and checked the weather with Flight Service. A small line of storms had formed between Jacksonville and Savannah. They weren't too severe, but did require an instrument flight plan. After Savannah, it was clear all the rest of the way.

I hurriedly cleaned up, grabbed breakfast in the coffee shop, and drove to the airport. After loading, turning in the car, and paying my FBO bill, I was taxiing out for takeoff by 0815. Daytona International was bustling already, mostly with Embry-Riddle training flights, but I soon got released and headed north.

I had filed for only 5000 ft, so I was being passed from one approach control to the next. A little north of Jacksonville, I started to encounter clouds, and one up ahead appeared to be pretty dark. I called Jax Approach and asked for deviation to the west. "I'm going to hand you off to Savannah in a few miles," came the reply. "Make your request to them."

I was hoping this would be soon. In a few minutes (but seemingly much longer), I was told to contact Savannah, but when I tuned in their frequency, I heard a lot of chatter. It seemed a Beech Baron had lost electrical power in the clouds and had declared an emergency. He must have been talking on a handheld unit. I kept waiting for a chance, and finally got a call in to them with my deviation request. He resumed talking to the Baron, then very quickly said, "Six three Juliet, turn left two nine zero!"

I rogered and turned just in time, as the dark clouds were right ahead and showing lightning. I got around them okay and broke out of the clouds altogether just north of Savannah. I remained IFR, though, all the way to Florence, just to be safe. The weather there was clear, but very windy and rough. Leaving there, I climbed up to 7,500 ft to top the turbulence and proceeded on VFR. I set the power for 75 percent according to my power schedule, and leaned to best power setting.

When I got up into West Virginia and Maryland, the fuel gauges started to look pretty low. The tailwinds were fairly weak, and it was taking longer than I figured. Still, I figured I had plenty of fuel based on timing. I consistently burned 10 gal/hr at 70 percent, and only a little more at 75. By the time I got into southern Pennsylvania, the gauges were showing empty, but I had flown less than 3.5 hours, and the tanks held about 4.5 hours worth of fuel. I pressed on, but got a little more concerned as I neared home base, because the gauges were pegged and not even bouncing.

I made it okay, though. When I got to the hangar, I called the fuel truck and watched the crew pump forty-three gallons into my forty-eight-gallon tanks. Boy, that was getting pretty low! I had flown about 3.75 hours, which worked out to 11.5 gal/hr.

A week later, I had the tachometer calibrated and found that the gauge was indeed off. I was actually doing 100 rpm more than the gauge indicated. No wonder I used so much fuel. I made note of this error in my power schedule for future flights. Unfortunately (or maybe fortunately), I never got to make good use of that information, because I never made any more flights of that length.

Most of my flying from then on was confined to trips of about 100 miles or less. I went to weekend fly-ins, to eatery spots for lunch, to give talks at various aviation events, or just to visit the guys at other airports. One such trip, however, turned out to be quite memorable.

On 9/11/2001, I was in the air when all aircraft were grounded because of the terrorist attacks on New York City and Washington. I had gone down to Kampel Airport near my hometown, which was owned by my old buddy, Larry. I had to deliver some photos from a recent class reunion, and then planned to have lunch with Larry. I had heard of the first crash into the Twin Tower before I had left University Park, but didn't think it was that serious.

When I got to Kampel, a group was gathered around the radio listening to the news, and I learned of the second Twin Tower attack, and the one on the Pentagon. As we listened, they announced the collapse of the towers. The newscaster then stated that there were "several crashes reported in western Pennsylvania." I turned to Larry, and said, "Something is really going on here. I better skip lunch and head for home as soon as I can."

He agreed, and I took off immediately. As usual, I tuned in Harrisburg Approach Control when passing through their airspace. I was somewhat surprised to hear no traffic on this usual busy frequency. Just as I was leaving their area, I finally heard a Cessna call in 20 miles west, and declare his intentions to land at Harrisburg Capitol City. "Capitol City is closed. Suggest you land at Carlisle," came the response.

Hmm, that's strange! I thought it probably had something to do with the attacks, but wasn't sure exactly what. I continued on and switched to 122.8, the common Unicom frequency. Again, all was silent. Usually on a nice day like that was, this channel would be buzzing with activity. About ten minutes later, I heard somebody somewhere warn a helicopter to exit the crash area because it was a crime scene. I began to get more concerned, and thought maybe we were under some general attack. I started to look diligently for enemy aircraft. Problem was, I didn't know who the enemy was.

As I neared University Park Airport, my home base, I switched to New York Center frequency, the controlling agency for IFR traffic in our area. Then I heard the warning, "Attention all aircraft this frequency, all civil aircraft flight is prohibited. You are advised to land at the nearest airport immediately."

Things were getting clearer. Since I had my transponder on, I figured they were talking to me (among others), but I made no response. I was close enough to UNV to consider it the closest, so I headed there (which I was doing anyway). Now, however, I got even more vigilant for other aircraft. In addition to watching out for enemy aircraft, I thought maybe American fighters would try to escort me out of the air (or worse).

I made my usual request to UNV for a traffic advisory, and got the usual calm reply from our faithful Unicom operator. She concluded with, "No other reported traffic."

Why did that not surprise me? I landed uneventfully, without encountering either enemy or friendly fire. The lineman who helped me put my airplane into the hangar, said, "Be sure to lock the gate when you leave."

I went up to the office and watched the news on the TV in the lounge. This was the first I learned the full details of all the day's events. I saw why I was asked to lock the gate. I was the last airplane to land at our airport that day, and the last operation for several days.

The ban on civil aviation was soon lifted, and flying resumed fairly quickly to nearly normal. We now had to contend with a new federal regulator, however, the Transportation Security Agency (TSA). In addition to the FAA, we now had to also satisfy the TSA that we were safe to fly.

My focus remained, though, on the medical aspects of the FAA requirements. Much of my summer was taken up with completing all the medical tests exactly as the FAA required them, gathering up records of all the tests and doctor's statements, and then putting all this together into a package to submit to the Aeromedical Center in Oklahoma City. After that, I would nervously wait to receive the decision as to whether I could continue to fly.

Then, in 2004, the FAA finally adopted the much-anticipated sport pilot category. Pilots operating under this category could fly light sport aircraft (LSA) with a valid driver's license in lieu of a medical certificate. LSAs were basically two-place, single engine airplanes with a maximum gross weight of 1320 pounds or less and a maximum speed of no more than 120 knots. In a few years, numerous new models were introduced in this category.

I studied these aircraft with great interest, examined them at the major air shows, and took demo rides in a number of them. Finally, in 2009, I had had enough of fighting for a medical and threw in the towel. I let my medical certificate expire and didn't apply for renewal. Instead, I began a concentrated search for a light sport.

I located a low-time, 2007 Tecnam Sierra in California. Tecnam is an old established Italian manufacturer headed by a rather noted aircraft designer. They make several models of LSA, and I had zeroed in on the Sierra as the ideal model for me. I arranged for it to be flown in for examination (for a fee). When I saw it and got to fly it, I was hooked. I bought it.

I put the Cherokee up for sale. Juliet had been with me for twenty-five years, and she had served me well. I always thought that it would be hard to part with her, but I knew the time had come to move on. A friend of mine who brokers airplanes sold the Cherokee in a few months.

The Sierra took some getting used to, but learning the little eccentricities of a new airplane was exciting and challenging. It gave me a renewed enthusiasm for flying. I also had a modern electronic flight instrumentation system installed, and learning to operate that and all the features it has was even more intriguing.

The airplane performs almost as well as the Cherokee. It is only a few knots slower, climbs even faster, and has the same range. As a sport pilot, I am restricted from IFR and night flight, but I can do just about everything else with this airplane that I did with the Cherokee. Like Juliet, the Sierra is growing close to my heart.

My last picture with Juliet.

The Sierra takes Juliet's place in my hangar.

Chapter Fifteen
Miscellaneous Memories

Through the years, there were numerous little incidents that stand out in my memory. One of the first tense situations that I encountered occurred with the Aeronca Chief shortly after I started flying it. On a nice Sunday afternoon, my buddy, Pete, and I had flown over to the Harrisburg Airport, just twelve miles away, to see what was happening there. Pete had a sleek, single-place Mooney Mite. He went in that, and I in the Chief. While chatting with some of the locals, we noticed clouds building up to the west, the direction of our home airport. "Maybe we should head back home," I said to Pete.

He agreed, and we took off a few minutes later. Climbing out, I had a better view of the clouds, and they looked even more ominous than they did on the ground. The Mooney was much faster than my Chief, so, after slowing to stay with me for a while, Pete throttled up, and pulled out ahead. After a short while, I saw him headed back toward me. I figured that he had assessed the weather and decided to head back to Harrisburg. But then he circled around behind me and again headed west. I interpreted this as a sign that it was all right to proceed on home. I had great faith in Pete. He was a very accomplished pilot. He had 400 hours flying time!

The storm (the better description of the clouds at this point) was approaching fast from the west, and we were in a race to see who got to the airport first. I could see lightning in the clouds by this time. As we got to the field, the windsock showed the wind right down the runway. Pete went straight in ahead of me, and landed far down the field, presumably to give me space behind him.

I headed straight in also, and as I neared the field, the wind got increasingly turbulent. The storm was really close, dark, and full of lightning. This was going to be a close one! I had never faced a really dangerous situation in the air before in my seventy-some hours of flying.

I bounced around quite a bit, but managed to get down okay. Then, just as I touched down, the wind suddenly shifted 90 degrees in a direct crosswind. Fortunately it was coming from the direction of the hangars. I quickly turned and headed into the wind. Then the storm hit! It really blew and poured rain.

At this point, I saw a bunch of guys running out from the hangar. Three of them grabbed the right wing strut and two grabbed the left. One of these was my old instructor, Grant. "Ease it in toward the hangar!" he yelled. "We'll try to hold you down!"

Then, suddenly, a really strong gust hit, and I felt us rise into the air. "Get the nose down, get the nose down!" Grant yelled.

I knew he didn't want us to stall, so I complied. I glanced out, and everybody was still hanging on, with their feet dangling a yard or so above the ground. Then we started to descend, and I flared just as in a normal landing, even though we were advancing forward only about 5 MPH. For a moment, we had been a six-place Aeronca!

No more strong gusts hit after that one, and we slowly proceeded to the hangar area. The guys were all soaking wet, and so was I after I shut down and jumped out to help push it into the hangar. I thanked them all profusely, and we went into the lounge to dry off.

Pete, in his low-wing Mooney, had climbed out and held the wing down himself until the brunt of the storm had passed, before taxiing in. The storm passed, and it cleared up nicely in less than an hour. In retrospect, it would have been much better to head back to Harrisburg and wait it out.

A few years later, at the same airport, I had bought the Ercoupe and was anxious to check out for night flying, since this airplane had an electrical system. I sought out an instructor one evening, albeit one of the more brash, young instructors who worked part-time there. Our little grass field had runway lights, but he suggested we fly over to the Harrisburg Airport, which had much better facilities for practicing night landings.

On the way over to Harrisburg, I switched on all the electrical equipment we had: nav lights, cockpit lights, two radios, and finally, the landing light, as we approached the airport. I didn't fully comprehend the load this put on my minimal electrical system, with its 15-amp generator and weak battery. As we rolled onto the runway on our first (and only) night landing, everything suddenly went dark.

We had been cleared to land, but I couldn't contact the tower for any further instructions. The instructor told me to exit at the next taxiway, and make my way to the ramp. It was difficult without a landing light to guide me, but I managed to creep in. As we neared the ramp, we got into a darker environment, and he spotted a yellow line. Thinking it was the taxiway centerline, he told me to follow it. All of a sudden, there was a crunching sound, and we came to a sudden stop. "We hit something," I said.

"We couldn't have," he responded. "We're in the middle of the taxiway."

"I don't care where we are," I argued, "we sure as heck hit something."

I shut down and we climbed out. It turned out that the line marked the edge of the ramp area, not the taxiway. We had taxied over a metal sign that indicated the designation of the taxiway, and the runway to which it led. It had dug into the belly.

We managed to push it back off the sign, and I started up and taxied on in until we came to a better-lighted area in front of the main hangar. I immediately went inside to a phone and called the tower to report what had happened. They didn't seem too upset about it. Then we checked the airplane over more carefully, and found the prop had gotten dinged up a bit as it passed over the sign.

The instructor said that it would be fine, and that we should just take off and fly home. Apparently, he wanted to avoid getting this incident on his record. I wanted no part of this. In addition to the banged-up airplane, we had no lights or radio. I insisted we leave it. So, we called the guys still around our home airport, and someone drove over and picked us up.

The next day, I went over to the shop at Harrisburg and arranged to have a temporary substitute prop installed, after which I flew it home for the belly repairs. I also went into the FAA district office on the airport and reported the accident. The manager didn't seem too concerned, and sent me out with a security guard to point out the damaged sign. It had only a few minor dents and scratches. I heard nothing further on the incident either from the airport or the FAA. I never sought the services of that flight instructor again, either.

After the night landing incident, the belly needed a new piece of skin about 1 by 3 feet in size. At the time, I worked as an engineer at nearby Olmsted AFB. A few days later, I went down to the sheet metal shop in the big repair hangar and asked the mechanics there if they had a scrap of .032 aluminum about this size. They were rather cold to this "necktie" that had disturbed them. "Necktie" was the term they used for someone from management or engineering who invaded their domain. "Naw, we don't have any scraps that big," was the curt reply.

One guy, however, was thoughtful enough to ask what I needed it for. When I told him it was for my own airplane, the foreman, or chief spokesman among them, said, "Oh, is this for a home job?"

When I replied in the affirmative, he turned to one of the other guys, and said, "Run over to the supply room and get a 4 by 8 sheet of .032 aluminum. We'll cut him a piece."

From then on, they were much more cooperative. Apparently, this somewhat unauthorized use of government equipment sort of separated me from a company man, and made me more one of them, even though I was a necktie.

In the summer of 1969, Patuxent River Naval Air Test Center in Maryland (known as Pax River) invited a faculty representative from various universities to spend several days touring the base and listening to presentations on the operations there. The purpose was to recruit future engineering employees. Our dean of engineering was one of the invitees. Since he was too busy, he passed the invitation on to our department head. He had another commitment also, so he asked me if I'd like to go, knowing this tour would be in my field. He told me to take the department Cherokee if I wanted. So, here was I, the junior assistant professor with an invitation that was initially given to the top official in the college.

It was possible to fly into the Naval base, but it took some paperwork, run through the correct channels. I looked at the chart and saw a small grass field airport, Park Hall, right outside the base. I called the contact at Pax and asked if someone could pick me up there if I flew in. He said that would be no problem, so off I went in 7PS on the day we were to assemble.

Park Hall was under the restricted airspace around the base, so the approach would be tricky. The procedure was to fly to a fix on the west bank of the Potomac, then proceed across the river at 600 feet or below. Believe me, trying to navigate VFR at that altitude wasn't easy, especially over open water. Nevertheless, I managed to find the airport.

It appeared to be more of a farm, with a landing strip cut out of it. There was a farmhouse, a barn, and a few small outbuildings, but nothing that resembled typical airport structures. I located a windsock, circled around, and landed.

The farmer was just driving in on his tractor, towing a load of hay. He stopped and walked over to me. I yelled out the storm window and asked if I could park somewhere for a few days. "Sure," he replied, "just follow me."

He walked over to where a Cessna and an old Comanche were tied down. They were parked in pretty high grass, and obviously hadn't flown in ages. He started kicking around in the grass next to the Comanche. I figured out that he was looking for tiedown ropes. Sure enough, he found two, and directed me over between them. I asked if there was a phone around to call Pax. "There's one in the kitchen, on the wall," he replied, pointing to the farmhouse. "Just walk in the back door, and help yourself."

He then went back to his tractor and proceeded with unloading the hay. After tying down and unloading my bag, I walked over, opened the screen door, found the phone, and called the contact at the base. Then I sat on the back porch and waited. A car pulled up in less than ten minutes.

When everybody got there, we were briefed and taken to a motel just outside the gate. The next few days were extremely interesting. We got to see the flight test facilities, the test pilot school, the simulated carrier deck, and many other fascinating activities. There was even a crab fest one evening. The only downside was that I was assigned a roommate who was a stuffy electrical engineering prof from NYU.

The day after things ended, I was given a ride to the airport. I didn't see a soul around, so I went up to the back porch and knocked on the screen door. A little teenage girl in a calico dress came to the door. She looked like the perfect role model for a part in State Fair, or something similar. I told her that I had been tied down there since Monday, and wanted to pay my tie-down fee, and whatever other charges there might be.

"Oh, we don't charge nothin'," she said. "We hardly ever get any visitors, and we're glad to have you."

I tried to insist, but she was firm in not charging me. So I loaded up, untied the Cherokee, and taxied out. The grass on the runway was not quite as high as the tie-down area, but it wasn't exactly short. I went to the very end of the field, put on some flaps, and ran up to full power before releasing the brakes. The old 180 Lycoming hauled me off well before the fence.

As I proceeded toward Washington, the air got increasingly hazy. I had no instrument rating at that time, so I decided to land at Dulles and assess the situation. Dulles had almost no airline traffic in those days, and was very friendly to general aviation. The weather got even worse north of there, so I tied down and called an old buddy of mine who lived in Arlington, just across the river from DC.

I stayed with him for a few days, but the extreme haze continued. By chance, that weekend was when Neil Armstrong and Buzz Aldrin landed on the moon. We stayed up to watch the landing, an emotional experience, as expressed very well by Walter Cronkite. My own thoughts were, *Geez, Neil Armstrong got to the moon, and I couldn't even get back to Pennsylvania!*

Some years later, Neil Armstrong was a professor at University of Cincinnati, and he was trying to start a flight test course. I had written a small lab manual for such a course. It wasn't much, but it was the only thing on that subject in print at the time. He wrote to me for a copy, and made a point of telling me to enclose a bill. Of course, I sent him a free copy. I included a note, stating, "Please accept with my compliments, my very small step for mankind."

A few years later, I made another trip to Pax River, this time to pick up an airplane. Lockheed had converted two Schweizer 2-32 gliders from the Naval Test Pilot School to powered airplanes for stealth operations in Viet Nam. A Continental O-200 engine was installed in each behind the cockpit, which was attached to a propeller shaft mounted overhead the cockpit through a gear-reduction V-belt drive. The shaft drove a four-blade, wide-diameter propeller at a very slow speed, thus reducing the noise output. The idea was to create a very quiet reconnaissance airplane that could be flown over enemy troops at night without detection. It was appropriately designated QT-2.

After an operational test in the battle zone, the airplanes were returned to the test pilot school at Pax. Only one was airworthy; the other was used for parts. A few years later, the Navy had no more use for the aircraft, so they offered the flying one to a university that could use it in some sort of flight research.

When Barney, my department head, got wind of this deal, he jumped at the chance to acquire a free airplane. He called me into the office one day, and informed me that we would fly down to Pax that Saturday, and I was to bring the QT-2 back. I wasn't too wild about the idea, but I thought it would be a unique experience. So, early that Saturday morning, we headed south in the Cherokee. Barney flew, and somehow had gotten permission to land right at the base.

On arrival, the tower warned us of an arresting cable a few hundred feet down the runway we were cleared to land on, but assured us that it was down. It was, but it rested on the runway surface, and was almost two inches thick. This situation didn't seem to bother the large wheels of the Navy aircraft that normally operated there, but when the Cherokee tires rolled over it, we got a jolt worse than that from any thermal I ever hit.

There was no damage, however, either to the airplane or to us, so we taxied to the test pilot school ramp, where we were met by a tall, serious-looking Navy instructor pilot. He took us over to the hangar for our first look at the QT. It was a really weird-looking airplane! We had been told that it was in very good condition, but in reality, it looked like a beat-up, war-weary bird. The fabric fuselage had a number of bullet holes, each of which was patched with a strip of duct tape. Apparently, the GI mechanics who maintained it in Nam were not very adept at fabric work.

The chief petty officer in charge of maintenance gave us a thorough briefing on the details of the bird, and what to look for in preflight inspection. He was particularly emphatic about making sure that all five V-belts were intact. We asked him where we could get a replacement if one was cracked. "Oh, Joe the Motorist, Pep Boys, any place like that," was his matter-of-fact reply.

Then it was check-out time, and I was selected to go first. I climbed into the front cockpit, with the instructor behind me. He started it up, and then told me to taxi. He communicated with the tower and directed me where to go.

The airplane had a stick control with a throttle on the left, similar to most tandem airplanes. In front of the throttle was the spoiler control from the original glider. There was a single bicycle wheel in the fuselage, also from the original glider configuration, with small outrigger wheels near each wingtip.

The ship leaned over on one outrigger. It was a weird way to taxi, especially on a large complex airport. As you turned to another taxiway, the outboard wing lifted up, and the bird flopped over on the other wing. We were guided out to a small runway by the bay, and cleared for multiple touch-and-go's. I was told to lock the spoilers in retracted position, and apply full power, as with any airplane. The lowered wing rose almost immediately, and it lifted off easily.

Near the end of the downwind leg, I was instructed to retard the throttle to idle, unlock the spoilers, and use them just like a throttle. If we were high, I would pull back on the control, increasing descent rate. If we were low, I would push forward, to decrease the descent. This was the standard procedure with gliders, as I was to learn later in formal glider training. I made a decent approach, and rolled the single wheel onto the runway. "Well, that wasn't too bad," my instructor said, in a tone that implied some degree of surprise.

We shot a few more landings, and then I was told to taxi to the ramp. It was the same weird flip-flop procedure that we used to go out. Then it was Barney's turn, and I went inside for a very welcome cup of coffee. After his checkout, we broke for lunch, and it was the first time all morning that Barney and I got to converse alone. "Hey, I don't think we want that airplane," he said very seriously. "The wing is wider than our runway."

He went on to express concern about the maintenance and other aspects. I was very glad to hear all this, since I felt much the same way. We broke the news to the officer in charge, who tried to convince us to take it, but Barney stood firm. The maintenance chief was even more disappointed. I got the impression that it had been a maintenance nightmare.

We climbed aboard the Cherokee and headed for home. This time, I flew, and I felt very relieved to be flying this familiar bird instead of the strange airplane I thought I was going to have to fly. I wondered if I would have even made it home in that.

Barney and I flew a lot together, and we got to be a well-coordinated team. On long trips with multiple legs, we would alternate the piloting duty. The other one of us in the right seat would set up radio frequencies, select the proper VOR's, and perform other navigation chores.

A popular trip was to the general aviation conference held in Wichita, Kan. every spring. On one such venture, I had flown the first leg to Shelbyville, Ind., and Barney took the second one, intended to be to Jefferson City, Mo. After we passed St. Louis,

I tried to tune in the Jefferson City VOR, but couldn't pick it up. Thinking we were too far out, I told Barney to continue going outbound on the St. Louis VOR. After multiple attempts, I told Barney that we weren't picking up Jeff City. He said, "Let me try contacting Jeff City tower."

That effort also failed. By now, we were getting pretty close, so we began to have some concerns. Barney kept trying the tower unsuccessfully. Then he said to me, "I think I see why we can't contact Jefferson City. Take a look over here."

He banked the airplane to the left, and, as I looked out the left window, I saw what he meant. The airport was totally under water! All you could see was the tower and the tops of some other buildings sticking out of the water. Flooding in the Midwest was common this time of the year, as snow melted in the northern regions.

I scanned the chart quickly, and saw Sedalia, just a little north of our route, was on higher ground, and appeared to not be near any water. I set up a course for there, and gave them a call on Unicom—they had no tower. They responded right away and informed us that they were open, and also had fuel. I told them we were running low, but thought that we could make it.

"We don't have a fuel truck," they advised. "You'll have to taxi to the pump. But if you run out on the ground, we can bring you a few gallons in the pickup truck."

Hey, this was the Midwest, where people are friendly and accommodating.

We made it okay, though—all the way to the pump. After refueling, I flew the next leg to Wichita without incident.

A few years later, I made this trip with Denny and Mark, two of our younger faculty members, and both pilots. On the return trip, Denny flew the first leg. I rode right seat, and Mark was in the back. With a good tailwind, we made it all the way to Terre Haute, Ind. As we taxied in toward the ramp, a fuel truck came out to meet us. When the truck stopped, a very comely young lady in tight shorts hopped out and directed us into a parking spot.

We all sat up and took notice of this sight. When we shut down, Denny opened the storm window and told her to fill both tanks. She climbed up on the truck, undid the nozzle, and proceeded to unroll the heavy hose as easily as any man. As she filled the one tank, we continued to just sit there and stare, mesmerized by this unexpected display of feminine pulchritude. Finally, Mark said, "I guess we could get out."

"Oh, yeah," I responded, realizing that I was by the door, and that it was my duty to unlatch it and initiate the egress.

We climbed out and proceeded into the terminal to look for a place to eat. Over lunch, we concluded that it was not a good idea to have such an attractive line service attendant. It was very distracting, and could possibly cause accidents.

One of my last instrument flights turned out to be somewhat disturbing, but could have ended up much worse. When I still had Juliet, I had dropped off my one nav/com radio for repairs at the avionics shop at Altoona-Blair Co. Airport, about forty miles to the south. Having been notified that it was ready, I set out for the airport to fly down and get it.

When I got there, though, the airport was all fogged in, although it was forecast to clear up soon. I hung around and had some coffee, but seeing the clearing to be much slower than expected, I decided to file an IFR flight plan. I went to the hangar, preflighted, taxied out to the end of the runway, and called New York Center for clearance. At that time, New York Air Traffic Control Center handled instrument traffic at our airport from their location on Long Island through local radar antennas.

Center read me my clearance, which was concluded with the instruction, "Hold for release."

This was a frequent instruction, due to their remote location, and the increasing IFR traffic from the three regional airlines that operated at University Park. I acknowledged, and then sat there patiently waiting for release. Suddenly, the controller said, in a rather urgent tone, "Six three Juliet, are you ready to go?"

"Affirmative," I quickly replied.

Then, "You're released!"

I figured he wanted me out as quickly as possible in order to clear another airplane to land, so I hurriedly acknowledged and taxied out onto the runway, turning to head down it as I went. At the last minute, I caught sight of two landing lights approaching out of the fog behind me. Uh-oh! What do I do now? I had to make a split-second decision. Would it be quicker to try to turn around and get back onto the taxiway, or to continue the takeoff and hope to get off ahead of the other traffic?

Since I was already rolling, I chose the latter and continued to apply full power. This proved to be unwise, because before I even reached flying speed, I heard the roar of twin turboprops overhead, and saw a United Airlines commuter pass over me. The pilot angrily reported that he was going around, and then said to Center, "I want the number of that airplane and the name of the pilot that cut me off!"

Center remained completely silent, as they should have. After all, it was really their goof. Since I had not helped the situation, I didn't say a word, either, except to acknowledge further ATC instructions. I continued on to Altoona without further incident.

By the time I got the radio installed, University Park had cleared up, so I came back VFR. As soon as I put the airplane away, I drove over to the airline terminal, went up to the United counter, and asked to see the local manager. I tried to explain to her just what happened and expressed my sincere apologies for disrupting their operations.

She told me that the captain was so upset because he had a company official on board coming in on business. Wouldn't you know it!

I gave her my business card and told her that the captain or anyone else in the company could call me if they wanted. I also filed a NASA Form 277. This is a voluntary action that is part of a NASA-FAA safety program for reporting incidents such as this. Doing so pretty much exonerates pilots from disciplinary action, unless, of course, it involves an accident or serious violation of the regulations. I didn't think I broke any regulation, but filing the report couldn't hurt.

I never heard a word from either United or the FAA.

As long as I had the Cherokee, which was instrument-equipped, and I had the credentials to fly IFR, I maintained my instrument currency, so that I could fly small trips such as this one. Now, operating as a sport pilot, I am no longer allowed to fly IFR. So, my instrument flying days are over.

I sort of miss that aspect of flying. I enjoyed working the system. It just seemed more professional to be interacting with ATC, and following their instructions as precisely as I could. I also liked the idea of being on a mission to a specific destination and experiencing the satisfaction of completing it under less-than-ideal conditions.

Nevertheless, I am happy to still be flying at all. The sport pilot/light sport aircraft rules came along at a most opportune time for me. They have enabled me to experience a different type of airplane. I had flown many airplanes as light as the Tecnam Sierra I now fly, but none with such excellent performance and handling. I am really enjoying getting to know this great little airplane and exploring its capabilities.

The QT-2 quiet stealth aircraft

Epilogue

When I reached the half-century mark of flying, the local district office of the FAA presented me with a "Wright Brothers Master Pilot Award" for fifty years of continuous, accident-free flying and many contributions to further the cause of aviation safety. Awardees are prominently displayed in a role of honor at FAA headquarters in Washington, D.C. I was very proud to receive this prestigious award, and considered it to be the climax of my flying career.

On the other hand, I didn't think that I really deserved it. I never thought of myself as a "master pilot," but rather as just an ordinary pilot, as the title implies. Looking back over the years, however, I realize that some of the adventures I describe are not really all that ordinary.